# Birth

# OF A SELF-CARE

# VIGILANTE

## TAP INTO THE UNIVERSE
## FOR RECOVERY: BOOK 1

## ILANA KRISTEVA

TAP INTO THE UNIVERSE FOR RECOVERY, BOOK 1:
BIRTH OF A SELF-CARE VIGILANTE™
By Ilana Kristeva

Paperback ISBN: 978-0-9963037-6-7
Electronic Book Text: ISBN: 978-0-9963037-0-5
Digital (format EPUB): ISBN: 978-0-9963037-1-2
Audio Book: ISBN: 978-0-9963037-2-9

Cover Superstar: Hermosa Beach Seagull of Hermosa Beach, CA, USA
Cover Photo: Yuriy Hristev
Book Design: Karrie Ross at karrieross.com
Back Cover Author Photo: Hope Harris at hopeimages.com

Field of Choices
(916) 246-6017
www.fieldofchoices.com

# DEDICATION

I dedicate this book to my mother, Joan Ying, who gave birth to me against all odds, and to people who live with chronic pain and addiction—and those who care for them.

ೞ

*In loving memory of*
*Ann Marie Ciesnewski, Mike "KRTH" Phillips,*
*Bradley Kolfschoten, Muriel Lahey, Mary Shumate,*
*May Lee, and Robin Williams—my merry band of*
*cheerleaders in the celestial realm—who have*
*made my recovery possible.*

# FOREWORD

Ilana Kristeva's story is a stirring inspirational account of the changes she made that led to her healing. Her journey holds nothing back. It is a testimonial of personal transformation from living with multiple illnesses and addictions to Self-Care Vigilante™.

As a psychotherapist and registered nurse in private practice, I have been observing and helping people for over forty years. With thirty years of my own recovery under my belt, I know the recovery field personally as well as professionally. I was very fortunate to work beside Dr. Earle Marsh, who was the first physician to get sober with Bill W. and Dr. Bob in the very early days of Alcoholics Anonymous. Dr. Marsh is the author of "Physician Heal Thyself," one of the stories in the "Big Book" of Alcoholics Anonymous.

Recovery from alcoholism and/or drug addiction is a difficult, lifelong process that requires deep, daily commitment to change. Ms. Kristeva's story of recovery from debilitating illnesses, severe pain, alcoholism, food addiction, compulsive spending, and massive denial is nothing short of a miracle.

All too often, well-meaning physicians gave up hope for her, a patient with Complex Regional Pain Syndrome (CRPS) and many additional illnesses, because medication and surgery could not cure her condition. Her complex issues baffled many people who wanted to help, but could not. She ended up in a wheelchair feeling crazy.

As someone who has struggled with physical issues myself and rehabilitated from major surgeries and temporary loss of mobility, I identified with Ms. Kristeva's battles. I have also witnessed how rare this kind of commitment to heal is and how unusual it is for a person with such severe problems to persevere, change her attitude, change her way of being in the world, change her thoughts, change her energetic patterns, and finally, heal her soul and painful, broken, sick body. Ms. Kristeva decided to get well and end her suffering.

Her next step was to take total responsibility for her situation and condition. This message of her healing journey is one of courage and hope to move beyond being a victim of addictions, pain, and circumstances into full physical, emotional, energetic, and spiritual healing. This book reveals her heroism, resolve, and determination to learn to listen to her own body, trusting that the right guidance and support would appear when she was ready for it.

She makes it clear that there is no exact formula for this kind of journey. It is intensely personal. In this book, she leads the way and points to the possibilities of healing with grace, courage, and humor. Her story can open the door to recovery for you, the reader, who may be trapped and victimized by forces you do not understand.

You. Can. Recover.

Best wishes on your journey,

Lynn Kennedy Baxter, R.N., M.A.
Licensed Marriage & Family Therapist
Author of *Make Exercise Easy with EFT & Instant Exercise Inspirations MP3* and *Make Exercise Easy: Frequent Flashes of Inspiration*

# TABLE OF CONTENTS

# Surrender and Victory

I was working on a very exciting personal project when something in my body suddenly forced me to drop everything and begin writing this book. The phrase "resistance is futile" echoed relentlessly through my head. Then, the face of Captain Picard from *Star Trek: Next Generation* came into my mind's eye. This blast from the past surfaced even after many years of not watching any *Next Generation* episodes or movies. It was not long before I discovered that this overwhelming flood of sound and imagery had appeared for a very good reason.

*Resistance is futile.* The message was clear: the Universe had designated this moment for me to write to you. I was in pain, but my migraine headaches and hypersensitivity to light began to dissipate soon after starting the first draft. Picture me wearing sunglasses and squinting at the computer to minimize the amount of light going into my eyes. Add swollen cheeks to the image, thanks to a crazy salivary gland infection. With both of my hands on the keyboard and my jaws clamped shut, I was not able to indulge in one of my very favorite pastimes—masticating. Chewing makes me happy. Now you know.

Gone are the severe migraine headaches, light sensitivity, and salivary gland infections. Following "orders" from the Universe created something wonderful. Surrender can lead to victory. I like that idea, and this book truly is proof of it. The more I wrote, the more vibrant I became. Although I resisted the idea of walking away from my personal project, doing so brought me to you—a terrific reason to follow guidance from the Universe!

When I first heard the words in my head—*resistance is futile*—I did not find it logical to share my healing journey in a book. To me, personal issues of health, gender identity, addiction, and other matters were private and nobody else's business. However, revealing my story brought me unexpected relief from physical misery, which then empowered me to bring to life the Universe's vision of a series of books, beginning with this one.

Wait—there is much more to this. Many years ago, I saw a movie in which everyone thought a doctor was crazy to believe that his catatonic patients, survivors of an encephalitis epidemic (inflammation in the brain), could be brought back to life. Filled with conviction, he patiently waited for the slightest glimmer of light in their eyes—or some sign of willingness to return to their bodies in response to his treatments. He knew deep in his soul that they could be reached. I so loved watching how earnestly he wanted them to wake up and continue celebrating their lives.

No one could have played this part in *Awakenings* (1990) better than Robin Williams. The fervor, compassion, and intensity that emanated from this genius profoundly affected me. When I found myself lying in the fetal position, buckled from endless pain with no known cure, it seemed as if chronic pain had dissolved my brain and left me catatonic. At times I was unable to communicate my needs to anyone or do anything for myself. Robin Williams' face was there for me, waiting with hope and beckoning me to come back just as he had done with the patients in the movie. This was yet another amazing message from the Universe.

Surrendering my old idea of keeping everything to myself led to countless surprising outcomes, including better health, exciting relationships, creative opportunities, and an overall sense of well-being in my body and on this planet. Every obstacle encountered in my journey of rebuilding this body lit a flame under my seat to engage with the world and find people and solutions in unlikely places, including ancestors who have long since passed.

I now open up my private world with hope that you will find awe in the priceless value of practicing daily self-care (self-compassion) and reaching out to the Universe for unlimited options to grow your inner garden. Build a daily self-care regimen that helps you rise above all distractions so that you may thoroughly enjoy the many talents and gifts with which you were born.

**Deliberate recovery is consciously follow-ing our gut intuition and taking bite-sized steps to invite life-affirming nutrients into the body,**

**mind, and spirit simultaneously, so that our natural talents and gifts may emerge when we follow our intuition—wisdom that arrives through our spiritual umbilical cord to the Universe.** Deliberate recovery works; connecting our collaborative teamwork of mind, body, and spirit (heart) to the Universe's unlimited power, grace, and love creates incredible results. Not only do we feel better in our bodies, but we also improve the health and safety of our communities. Sooner than later, we can receive a higher return on investment in ourselves through robust self-care regimens that offer us greater pleasure, purpose, and prosperity.

Believe it or not, you can access the great energy and wisdom that vibrate within and beyond your body to enhance every area of your life. Anything we can or cannot see contains energy that vibrates its own unique pattern (Law of Vibration). Choose to surrender old ideas that no longer serve you and dial into your gut intuition; all will benefit from your actions in one way or another. **Start now. Grant yourself permission to take deliberate actions that help you flow more smoothly throughout the day while allowing broken bones, hearts, and dreams to heal and grow.** Tap into your connection to the Universe's unlimited source of energy, knowledge, and forgiveness. Receive new perspectives on overcoming your health challenges, financial ups and downs, and roadblocks with people, circumstances, and change. Become a role model for your loved ones and see them awaken from the presence of a guiding light within you.

I am writing this for you: someone who perhaps suffers from chronic pain, illness, or addiction, and might also experience a sense of hopelessness or lack of purpose on this planet. You may have felt either detached from or extremely frustrated with your body, for whatever reason, and have faced seemingly endless cycles of ups and downs in many areas of your life. Perhaps you have loved deeply and devoted immeasurable time and energy to healing other people's wounds, solving their problems, and being the person that would never forget or abandon them. While doing so, you have abandoned your own body, your dreams, and your passions. It is no wonder that exhaustion has plagued you! At this moment, I encourage you to put yourself first; read this book and enjoy sharing it with others from a place of plenty, gratitude, and joy.

Join me on this journey. May my "a-ha" moments offer you hope and my struggles give you a glimpse into why you—and perhaps your loved ones—may be struggling. Accept that no matter what is happening all around you, you can take meaningful action in gaining physical and emotional comfort, safety, and stability in your own body. **Feeling rock-solid, you can offer so much more to others when energy, information, and strength from your connection to the Universe flow continuously through you.** Practice compassion toward yourself. Be a stunning role model. Deliberate recovery works. Live *on purpose*, not by default. Keep "good vibrations" alive to help you flow easily throughout the day.

You have plenty of time for everything the Universe deems necessary for your mission on Earth. Begin making peace with all parts of your body and reclaim your life so that you may thrive (not just survive) and serve others with vibrant energy and pure intentions. Allow this book to support you. With your eyes on these pages, breathe in deeply through your nose and breathe out gently through your lips if you can every time you see this symbol: **CB**. Replenish your body with water and be "one" with the great oceans of our planet.

At the end of each chapter, ponder on the mindfulness meditation passages or tap on your meridian points for release and relaxation. Receive guidance from a practitioner or therapist with experience in Emotional Freedom Technique (EFT) or Progressive Energy Field Tapping (Pro EFT™). Honor your memories, emotions, and thoughts and embrace all parts of your mind, heart, and body. Allow my *7 Key Ingredients for Vibrancy* and *26 Self-Care Vigilante Affirmations* to inspire your success in moving energy within your body, to release stuck energy and toxins, and to bring about change in your home, work, and other environments.

Taking better care of yourself impacts not only your time on earth but also the lives of others on this planet and everything beyond. Living with chronic pain, illness, or addiction can be a touchstone of spiritual growth that invites more happiness into your world—and that of your future generations. I ask you to seize any bit of hope for a better life that includes well-managed pain and wide-open doors to new opportunities. Take personal responsibility for the quality of every breath, thought, and action to overcome your perceived obstacles. Be a powerhouse of energy, a connector between the vast Universe (or heaven) and Earth.

*Recommit to being here on this planet with a self-care regimen that sharpens your gut intuition and strengthens your immune system, so that you may rise above life's many distractions and share your laughter and talents with the world.*

It truly is a choice.
Grant yourself permission to SHINE!

ଔ

*"I choose to pace myself gently, like a marathon runner, so that I may glide across the finish line in all areas of my life with grace, ease, and laughter."*
—Ilana Kristeva

# Birth

## OF A SELF-CARE

# VIGILANTE

TAP INTO THE UNIVERSE
FOR RECOVERY: BOOK 1

CHAPTER ONE :

# I Am on the Bridge

## My Bridge

I am standing in the middle of a very long bridge. Do you see me? This is a bridge that connects the world of traditional Western Medicine (W.M.) and the ancient wisdom and practices of my ancestors from China. Although I had never intended to be on this magnificent piece of architecture, my gratitude for it is immense and immeasurable.

Since the day I was born, doctors of W.M. have saved my life many, many times. With a history of anemia, allergies, asthma, and other serious conditions, I was accustomed to being in the middle of wailing sirens and emergency rooms by the age of twelve. Syringes, IVs, and oxygen masks were my best friends. They granted me access to continue breathing on this planet.

About eight-and-a-half years ago, I suddenly did not know who to turn to when I saw the looks on the faces of two orthopedic surgeons, a podiatrist, and a pain-management physician. They stared at my foot and shook their heads as they confirmed my diagnosis: Complex Regional Pain

Syndrome (CRPS), which is also known as Reflex Sympathetic Dystrophy (RSD). There is no known cure for my condition as of yet—only treatment that might reduce the pain I will likely face for the rest of my life. CRPS is an illness—more specifically, a chronic inflammatory disorder of the nervous systems. In simpler words, my nerves have *gone bonkers* and are out of control. This disorder affects at least one area of the body and potentially spreads to all limbs (feet/legs and hands/arms) and, in some cases, the entire body (full-body CRPS).

Thus far, my progressive illness has affected three of my limbs. It began in my right leg, during the recovery of a foot fracture, ankle injury, and hip labral tear. Within a year and a half, my entire left leg began to mirror the right leg, including muscle atrophy and even greater skin sensitivity, among other symptoms. A few years later, my entire right shoulder and arm, down to my hand, began to mirror some of the symptoms, but without the intensity that disabled both legs.

Without oversimplifying my condition, I use the analogy of a broken fire-alarm system to describe my understanding of what is happening in my body. My sympathetic nervous system has the job of pulling the lever of the fire alarm (clang, clang, clang) to warn my body of *DANGER*. When I rolled my ankle and fractured my foot while helping a client in a wheelchair, my sympathetic nervous system served me well; the pain was so intense that I was not able to put any weight on my right leg.

However, my parasympathetic nervous system was unable to do its job of turning *off* the alarm after the initial injury. We could say that it did not receive the announcement that the danger is now over. My conscious mind knows that the threat to me is gone, but the "stop button" for the alarm is broken. In short, there is a ton of noise going on in my body, and it wreaks havoc on all the other systems, with miscommunicated messages flying everywhere. This is one circus tent you do not want to enter. There is no laughter here.

CRPS set into my body and rocked my world as if having fibromyalgia and hypermobility syndrome were not enough. The Universe needed my undivided attention, but I had not been sitting still enough to listen. Before the chronic-pain circus came to town, I used to be a very sharp, intelligent, and articulate person. The severity of the pain was so intense that my I.Q. must have dropped at least eighty points. Although not clinically diagnosed, I became delusional. Talking to the nails on the wall in my home, I insisted that they tell who had moved them. No one else was around to do such a thing, and I certainly could not have reached them from my bed or wheelchair. Having discussions with objects like the nails on the wall became my life— a life over which I had no control.

With CRPS symptoms spreading into other parts of my body, pain drained my energy level and left me exhausted but continuously searching for that next possibly more comfortable position, if even for only a few minutes. Ah, it was like searching for an oasis in the desert—no water and no palm tree. But I kept my hopes up for that illusive comfy position. Moving my body hurt; not moving my body hurt. Inside me, I was screaming, gasping, and screaming some more. You get the picture. ☙

## Ancestors on My Bridge

At some point after hours, days, weeks, and months of continuous pain, I began to hear voices and see the images of my ancestors who had died decades ago. Their spirits floated toward me and revived my childhood memories of them. Imagined voices and images or not, they brought me comfort I had never felt before. Alive in my mind again were videos, my memories of their meditation exercises, levitation, and movement of their bodies and internal energy. In Mandarin Chinese, this energy is known as *Chi* (pronounced "Ch-ee," or "Kee" in Japanese).

Having buried these images and sounds long ago, I spent much of my life holding on tight to only the world I could see, hear, touch, or feel. However, the severity of my physical pain blew a hidden door wide open, one that granted me access to a special sector of my memory bank, through which I then gained insight and wisdom in knowing how to proceed with my physical recovery. Through stories in this book and in subsequent books, you will see how these gifts have served me well, including incredible courage to walk through so many unknown passages.

On this bridge, I no longer ignore the wisdom of the spirit world and can embrace everything I am unable to see with the naked eye or grasp with the conscious mind. Neither intellect nor willpower could overcome the torment of chronic pain and patterns of self-sabotage. This was a hard pill to swallow in that I had always favored scientific evidence, as I come from a family of engineers and mathematicians—basically number crunchers. An atheist for about 33 years of my life, I began my career as an evangelical atheist on a soapbox during my pre-school days (this story coming soon). "Mind over matter" was one of my mantras, and according to this belief, I should have been able to wipe out my pain if I concentrated long and hard enough. As a small child, I used to close my eyes and "use my powers" to change the colors of traffic lights by sheer force of will. Sooner or later, those red lights always turned green, and my belief system remained safe and intact. *SIGH.*

Today, I truly embrace the non-visible, non-touchable world. Practically every cell in my body calls me to pay attention to what I cannot see with my human eyes. I respond with respect, love, and mindfulness of Chi within me. It is undoubtedly connected to a much larger, fantastic source of power that allows me to feel, touch, and move what I am physically unable to see. That power is definitely greater than myself, for it rotates the earth on its axis. I do not. It moves our planet to orbit the sun. Again, I cannot take credit for that. But if I ever do, just give me a nudge and put my ego in check. Today, I believe in God and make no apologies for doing so. My Creator ROCKS and helps me find my way out of pain. Yours can as well.

Overcoming the insanity of the chronic-pain circus in my body has been an unfolding gift given by a source that is far beyond me. The Universe is way more than stars, planets, and galaxies. It is energy within and beyond that connects all of us. I have no doubt about that, but if you do, just borrow my confidence for now, fasten your seatbelt, and expect to be surprised.

## Arrogance in the Pain Equation

Does a person really need to end up bedridden or in a wheelchair before developing a deeper relationship with her or his internal organs? In my case the answer was "Definitely yes!" I was as stubborn as a mule. In hindsight, I made mules look good. Do you remember the story about the race between the tortoise and the hare? It ended with the tortoise winning the race and leaving the hare completely stunned. Like the rabbit, my thinking was ridiculous, as I believed that fast and furious hopping would always get me across the finish line first. Overly self-confident—and seemingly self-sufficient, I might add—the hare took a nap during the race and woke up too late. The steadfast tortoise won the race.

I related to that arrogance, because my self-worth was based on the assumption that

I would always be able to do things my way, never needing help, and win the race. But deep bouts of depression plagued me when I could not put weight on my two feet, keep my balance, or walk. After some progress in my legs, inflammation in my wrists and hands showed me new levels of depression, shock, and hopelessness. I could not even slice my own onions. And then, I lost my voice. Not being able to talk whenever I wanted to—pardon my language—*pissed me off* and blasted my self-esteem to bits. Simple tasks, like getting myself to the bathroom or picking up something I had dropped on the floor, were painstakingly slow processes. At times, swallowing my own saliva was my great accomplishment for the day, aside from inhaling and exhaling, which is no small feat for someone with asthma. ☙

To cross the finish line like the tortoise, however, I had to ask others to be with me on this muddy road. What?!? Let people see me like this? *GULP.* I had to let go of my pride and arrogance. Self-isolation was not serving me well. Overwhelmed by my complex tower of health conditions, I was a sinking ship. Feeling insignificant and humiliated, I eventually made the decision to stop seeing myself as a victim and began taking action toward achieving the results I wanted. Dropping the baggage of self-pity was absolutely necessary to accomplish anything and everything I desired. Nice idea, but not so easy to achieve.

For a short while I did accept that my bones, ligaments, and tendons needed rest in order to heal and return to their original state. Unfortunately, I was completely unprepared for the intense axe-slicing, knife-twisting, explosive burning, incessant stinging, nail-driving, aching pain from the tip of my right toes to my hip. Former soldiers, nurses, athletes, dancers, and others know this pain all too well. ⌀

## Isolation in the Pain Equation

The reason you may not have heard of CRPS or RSD is that many of us who suffer from this condition have remained almost completely unseen, lying in the fetal position and drugged up on painkillers at some point in our journey. Many of us spend a lot of time nearly or completely naked. Our skin is so sensitive that even the softest of fabric feels like sandpaper. We are extremely sensitive to everything, including heat, touch, water, and clothing. On a good day, we might be able to wear specialty socks and very loose shoes to accommodate the fluctuation of extreme temperature and the size of our feet—from fire-hot swelling (edema) to ice-cold shrinkage at any given moment.

My years of needing to use crutches, wheelchairs, walkers, and double canes offered me the priceless opportunity to see how much I had taken for granted the legs and feet beneath me. After some time, people on legs began to look funny to me. They ran around like teenagers missing cellphones— without a clue as to how easy it is to lose our ability to walk. One morning I was on two legs, but by afternoon, I was *barely* on one. It happens.

As if being unable to walk was not challenging enough, I had migraine headaches that made me fantasize about detaching my head to save my body. Not only were sunlight and indoor lamps too bright for my eyes, even the lights from my cell phone, computer, and TV were too painful to tolerate. With these headaches, carpal tunnel syndrome flare-ups in both of my wrists made using walkers and canes impossible. Time and time again, my wheelchair and toilet-seat riser became my best friends.

Most basic everyday tasks were extremely challenging and took forever, it seemed. Using the toilet, preparing and eating food, getting dressed and undressed, using my cell phone, and opening doors were all huge feats that left me exhausted, frustrated, and hating life. Narrow doorways, malfunctioning door openers, and out-of-the-way accessibility ramps for disabled persons challenged me to find kind thoughts during my struggles with them. Many different types of packaging, especially food packaging, forced me to be an out-of-the-box engineer in figuring out how to unwrap (with painful hands) the layers of plastic, carton, foil, string, metal, foam, and more. People with healthy hands truly have no idea how good their lives are until they cannot use them. ❧

## Icing on the Pain Cake

The icing on this CRPS pain cake, for me, was losing my voice and wondering if I would ever hear it again. This was on top of having severe congestion in my nasal passages, sinuses, and throat. One day, after having lived with CRPS for four-and-a-half years, I saw the amazed look on my ear, nose, and throat (ENT) specialist's face. It spoke volumes as he struggled to re-open my blocked nasal passages. What an intense ordeal! He then discovered that I had laryngopharyngeal reflux, better known as "Silent Reflux." My stomach acid was eroding my esophagus (the food tube) and spilling into my larynx (the voice box). He showed me the damage to my esophagus and vocal cords through a fiber-optic camera inserted up my nose and down into my throat; it was no easy task, I assure you. Viewing this video feed left me dumbfounded and speechless (no pun intended). ⊗

Although I did not know exactly what to do with this nightmare of mine, I acknowledged, accepted, and embraced the diagnoses as part of my personal growth experience: getting educated without having to go to medical school. However, this business of not having functioning vocal cords went far beyond what I could handle emotionally. Physiologically, I was unable to moan, groan, rant, or rave. Having inflammation in other parts of my body was annoying enough. Dealing with swollen tissues in my breathing passages and larynx was downright dastardly. For a very brief moment, I did enjoy *not* talking. However, losing my ability to speak when I truly needed to was far beyond frustrating. With utmost eloquence, I can say, "It sucked."

This lesson was a good one though, for I learned that happiness in my nasal passages and sinuses depended upon happiness in my small and large intestines. Foods like cheese and other dairy products irritated my intestines and subsequently inflamed my sinuses. Certain foods in my stomach, like avocado, chocolate, onions, and other histamines, sent food back up my throat and eroded my esophagus while constricting my airway. I was not a pretty sight, inside or out, and just the thought of giving up some of my favorite foods killed what little joy I had left.

One night, at the point of complete exasperation, I negotiated with the Universe:

*O.K. I admit I took for granted the precious voice you gave me. There were many opportunities in which I could have used my voice and talents, but I hid them from everyone. If I ever get my real voice back, I promise to speak my truth, sing again, and use it for whatever message you wish me to share.*

Again, surrender leads to victory. Now you have the story of how and why this book and audiobook series came to be. The Universe gave me back my original voice. To fulfill my part of the deal each and every day, I use my voice with sincere willingness to carry the message of whatever the Universe deems necessary.

Looking back, I would say that my having been diagnosed with vocal cord dysphonia (VCD) was the tallest mountain but also the greatest gift among all my health conditions. Because I wanted to hear my voice again, eat without choking, and breathe freely without tightness, I had to take personal responsibility for every bit of food or liquid that went into my mouth. Regaining my voice would have never happened if I had continued eating the foods that were eroding my esophagus, irritating my intestines and stomach, and fogging up my brain.

It truly was a rough ride, as I had always wanted to eat *whatever I wanted* and lots of it, even when my stomach was already full. Working with two nutritionists, I eventually learned how to communicate with my internal organs and respond to their needs. Not only did my organs reveal what they liked and did not like, they also gave me feedback on when and how much to eat and which combinations helped them function best. This priceless relationship grew as I continued to "dial into my *Dan Tian*" (pronounced *dahn tee-en*), the area below my belly button and location of my "second brain," where I received wisdom from the Universe and source of all knowledge. Following my gut intuition truly reaps rewards.

One day, while sitting before one of my nutritionists, I shared the story of the chocolate-covered macaroon. At a friend's baby shower, I heard the plate of chocolate-covered macaroons calling my name. Like a faithful servant I went over to the table and picked up two of these cookies. As I bit into this coconut delight, my mouth suddenly spit out the bite onto my plate! My body did not want this, even though it tasted exactly like the 150 macaroons (same brand) I had eaten prior to that day.

Upon hearing the story, my nutritionist nearly fell off her stool from laughter. At last, the sugar addict (moi) had mastered the art of subconsciously rejecting what her body did not need. My body's brain served me well when the brain between my ears could not. Miracles really do happen.

Facing my "veritable cornucopia of high-octane maladies" (*Psych*, Season 6, Episode 6), I began developing healthy communication with my internal organs to overcome symptoms of fatigue; brain fog; tender trigger points; mood swings; difficulty breathing through my nose, windpipe, and lungs; manic-hyperactivity; depression; ringing in my ears; allergies; light sensitivity; pounding headaches; locked vocal cords; needle-pricking and shooting sensations; skin rashes and blisters; easily dislocated joints; stomach irritation; constipation (my favorite); and others with more interesting names. I also learned to manage the many CRPS symptoms before they completely managed me: axe-chopping pain, skin hypersensitivity with peeling and discoloration (dark maroon-black), muscle atrophy, irregular hair growth, incessant fluctuations between fire-hot burning/swelling and almost frostbitten cold feet, plus grinding pain deep in both of my hips. ☙

In hindsight, I am grateful for everything that happened, because it was through my body that I gained an amazing connection with a generous and powerful source in the Universe. You can bet that, like a respectable drama queen, I did my fair share of emotional vomiting with each new diagnosis. But in 12-step programs I learned to vent for only a short while, as we need to "get out of the problem and get into the solution," so to speak. And to avoid analysis paralysis, we do not have to pursue all the answers to the question "Why?" For everything that happens, there is a reason, and for everything that does not, there is a reason as well. The wisdom lies in my *not demanding* to know why things do or do not occur. I am to pay attention to what the Universe needs me to do and when and how to serve. Essential knowledge, people, and resources will come. My job is to trust.

As I strive to build more trust in my body each day, I want my body to have faith in me to do what is best for it at any given moment. Becoming more reliable, consistent, and accountable to my body improves my relationship *with you*—and your loved ones as well. The more collaboration that goes on within my body-mind-spirit team, the easier I relate to the world—with less anxiety, anger, and angst. This sounds good, and it feels good.

Trusting the wisdom of the Universe to carry me through all physical and mental health challenges was critical to my rehabilitation. Many years ago, I made a decision not to use any form of narcotic pain medication or medical marijuana as treatment for chronic pain. It was my belief that whether or not they were legal, I had no business touching them. When I stumbled into 12-step recovery, I pledged to stay sober from alcohol and any substance that could help me "go numb" or escape from reality. Although pain drove me nearly insane, taking medications that could make me "high" would have resulted in my getting locked up in a room, bouncing off the walls and drooling all over myself. Even some of the non-narcotic pain medications I tried made me feel loopy, drunk, hyper, sad, intelligent, *and* worthless—all within just a few minutes. Not sexy at all. ⚘

My determination and persistence in seeking other solutions to find relief opened up so many doors to splendor on Earth. Allow me to clarify that I am not against prescribed narcotic medications, but they are not for me. Just the thought of possibly suffering from withdrawal symptoms while weaning off meds gives me chills and nightmares. I am so grateful for the methods that continue to offer me long-term solutions without complications from physiological or emotional cravings. As long as I am on this planet, the world is a much safer place with a "clean and sober" me in it. Promise.

### What This Can Mean for You

Moving about on this long and beautiful bridge, I am not alone. It is a bridge that closes the gap between traditional Western medicine and Eastern wisdom. I am deeply grateful to have had many insightful and loving people alongside me. Several doctors helped me to take this great step when they looked me in the eye and said that modern medicine had not yet found a cure for my conditions. Their brutal honesty propelled me to seek solutions from a wide spectrum of healthcare professionals and healing practitioners. My strange but powerful experiences with insightful energy workers deepened the welcoming of ancestral spirits into my modern world. ○3

Today, I now enjoy astounding mental clarity and serenity, with fewer symptoms and drastically reduced pain. The process of stretching far beyond the limits of my conscious mind has delivered greater self-confidence and prosperity in all areas of my life. What a truly amazing gift! I dare say that the brain between my ears is healthier and more alert than before the tornado of illnesses hit me. And clean energy flows through my other brain (gut) or *Dan Tian*, where I connect with the Universe through a spiritual umbilical cord that continuously feeds information and wisdom into my body. Following my gut intuition transforms my easily distracted attention span into laser-sharp focus, with timely responsiveness. This is only the beginning.

I am able to see clearly and fulfill my purpose on this planet because of the wisdom, serenity, and prosperity I access through my intimate connection with the Universe. Welcoming new opportunities to bring ancient Eastern practices into the present, I now find life very appetizing and promising. Taking a great leap of faith—with a commitment to action—brought me here. Thus far, every minute of what I have put into this journey has been highly worthwhile. The big "WOW!" for me has been that even my perceived setbacks have propelled me forward.

Do yourself a favor and start now. Pay attention and nurture your mind-body-spirit connection so that you may thrive in all ways throughout your stay on this planet. You could take a leap of faith and make a commitment to building a solid team within you that works happily and collaboratively—conscious mind, body (subconscious mind), and spirit (heart). Investing in yourself does require taking splendid care of yourself today, and you will need to make the time and effort and spend money. Which would you prefer: pay now or pay *more* later? Be a Self-Care Vigilante by looking inward to your body for wisdom and actively responding to its needs. Feel the self-propelling power of this choice, like I do. Own it—for your sake and mine. Make a difference in the lives of generations before and after you by starting with YOU.

There is that other choice: start later or never. Perhaps you prefer to get old quicker. Hurry up and procrastinate on this, blame your problems on bad genes or the unfair world, and do not take personal responsibility for releasing toxic substances, thoughts, and energy in your body, mind, and heart. How does that sound? With this choice, you must begin putting money aside *right now* for hiring someone to clean, feed, and dress you sooner than you think. Why? Because there is a really good chance that you will not be able to do these things in the future if you are neglecting yourself now. Maybe you like the thought of having someone wipe your butt for you prematurely. If that is the case, do not look my way. I am nice, but not that nice. Are we intimate yet? ☯

I have a tendency to think that everything is all about me, which is actually true in most cases. However, my wanting to be able to wipe my own butt for many years to come is more than a personal ambition. I am forecasting a national crisis within the next twenty years. The broader impacts of self-neglect, sleep deprivation, malnourishment, pee and poo issues, road rage, domestic violence, and various forms of intoxication will create this national crisis. A significantly large population, the baby boomer generation (born 1946 to 1964), is now comprised of 50- to 70-year-olds. Less than twenty years from now, we will begin to experience a shortage of able-bodied caregivers in the United States who can provide support services to 70- to 90-year-old baby boomers plus younger generations of crystal-meth heads, bath-salt snorters, and junk-food junkies already losing control of their bladders. It will not be a pretty sight when we have to witness fewer people managing the toilet activities of many. Wrap your head around that one.

Now back to me. My wonderful future includes admiring healthy buttocks, but not cleaning them— except for my own, of course. Striving to keep my internal organs happy and healthy will help me get there. Most baby boomers I have met appreciate my choice in lifestyle and are currently seeking solutions for their arthritis, diabetes, dementia, addictions, and other ailments. However, people who still "nourish" their bodies excessively with energy drinks, sugar, processed foods, household chemicals, home-lab-created concoctions, prescription medications, and street drugs had better prepare themselves for a very steep uphill climb. If I were a gambler, I would bet that these generations will need care attendants far sooner than they even dare to imagine. How sexy is that? Not for me, thank you.

## Request for Collaboration

The statistician in me instinctively knows that we will be in short supply of resources to meet the simultaneous high demand for medical attention and care attendants to support both older and younger generations. Whether we like it or not, that era is coming very soon. How can we change the direction in which we are headed? One way is to take personal responsibility for our own well-being and integrating more self-care activities into our daily lives. **Self-care is the daily practice of inviting inspirational thoughts that ignite action toward developing, protecting, and growing a mind-body-spirit connection with the Universe.** In doing this, we express compassion for ourselves, which then empowers us to serve others. Being vigilant about living the principles and applying the wisdom and tools we learn, we become healthy role models and symbols of hope for others. Simply put, "Let it begin with me," you, and us!

I am asking you to join me on this bridge that connects traditional Western medicine with Eastern wisdom and everything in between. Let me know that you are here with a vibrant smile that comes from within you. Whether you are traveling near, alongside, or ahead of me, I thank you for your presence. My hope is that many more collaborations will form to allow real solutions and true Light to emerge. We are approaching a dimension in time that calls for us to close the gap. Together, we can attain higher levels of *good vibration* by adopting the principles behind my *7 Key Ingredients for Vibrancy* in this book. The principles of honesty and responsibility, mindset and guidance, release and flow, unity and proximity, self-compassion and time abundance, purpose and plenitude, and a self-care vigilante consciousness will take us far.

*Let us integrate spiritual principles into intellectual inventions and promote their practical application from the moment we wake up to the second we fall asleep.*

Look where you are now and how you envision yourself serving in years to come. Are you taking action to live fully in the present so that you may evolve into a person who serves with joy and prosperity? Allow the Universe's divine guidance to take you places and show everything that is within you. May all that you do, touch, and love flow with grace, ease, and heartfelt laughter. Take a deep breath now and begin our first exercise! ○ʒ

# Exercise for Chapter One

*Ilana's Mindfulness Meditation and Tapping*
*Exercise for EMOTIONAL BODY COMFORT in a*
*5-Part Format (adapted Progressive Energy Field*
*Tapping or Pro EFT\*)*

Here are passages you may reflect on as you breathe deeply (**CЗ**) in silent meditation or say the words aloud while relaxing and tapping together the SIDES of both palms of your hands—the "karate chop point" (KC Point). (*See APPENDIX A: Tapping Meridian Points.*) For tappers, you may refer to APPENDIX B for an Expanded Version of this exercise for Chapter One.

Reversal Neutralization is a very effective Pro EFT tool for calming down energy in your body that may be scrambled or flowing in the wrong direction. Say the "Reversals" aloud while you tap on the KC points, but note that neutralizing the scrambled energy is just the beginning of the tapping process for resolving complex issues—physical, emotional, or financial. It is a great start for relaxation. To have a full and fantastically freeing tapping experience, please seek guidance from an EFT or Pro EFT practitioner or from a psychotherapist who uses tapping.\*\* Do select someone you feel can support you in rising to new levels of self-discovery!

REMEMBER: Please drink some water before, during, and after this exercise. This is a vital part of cleansing and refreshing your body.

❖ Reversal 1: "Even though my frustration and disappointment in my body's lack of cooperation is keeping me from getting pain relief and good sleep, there's a part of me that is not ready to let it go, for whatever reason. (Maybe I'm an unlucky person, I'm being punished, or I did this to myself and deserve it.)*** But I want to love, accept, and respect myself anyway." ଔ

❖ Reversal 2: "Even though my agitation and anxiety about my condition and pain is blocking me from truly relaxing and healing in peace, I honor the part of me that's not letting it go and thank my body for telling me it needs my help. And I love, accept, and respect myself." ଔ

❖ Reversal 3: "Even though this pain, anxiety, and fatigue in my body is still holding me back from moving forward in different areas of my life, I thank my body for carrying me this far and ask it to forgive my impatience. I love and accept myself and offer the tender love and care I need and deserve." ଔ

❖ Reversal 4: "Even though this remaining discomfort in my body, mind, and heart has held me back from saying "Yes" to wonderful opportunities in my life, I choose to let go of my stress, anger, and fear and find courage, hope, and laughter. I embrace my "insides" and "outsides," because I love and accept myself deeply and completely." ଔ

❖ CHOICE Statement: "I *choose* to expand the energy within my body and envision my powerful heart in action, so that I may glow with vibrancy and confidence. Thank you, Universe, for *allowing* my inner light to attract beautiful opportunities, *nourishing* my body, heart, and soul with vibrant energy, and *empowering* me to be of service to myself and others. And I deeply and completely love and accept myself." ℃

*\*Pro EFT™ (Progressive Energy Field Tapping™) and the process of reversal neutralization or "Reversal Setup" were developed by EFT Master Lindsay Kenny.*

*\*\*Note to EFT and Pro EFT practitioners and mental health professionals. Although my story of personal transformation is the focus of this book, you can look forward to a forthcoming clinical (yet lively) workbook with a workshop that dives more deeply into many of the complex issues I bring to light. Thank you for dedicating your life to bringing relief to people living with chronic pain, illness, or addiction, as well as those who love and care for them.*

*\*\*\*You may wish to fill in a couple of your own possible reasons in any of these passages.*

# Birth of a Contrarian

## Obvious Confusion

Allow me to take you to the delivery room of the hospital where I was born. I came out of my mother's belly kicking and screaming the words, "I don't want to" (rebelliousness), "Leave me alone" (isolation), and "I'll do it myself!" (self-reliance). The doctor and nurses in that room were not enamored with my sage-like wisdom. Apparently, they were distracted by something else: I was missing three important body parts in my lower hemisphere—a bat and two balls! Before I was born, my parents had been told that they were having a baby boy. But the medical folks were wrong, kind of.

My mantras of rebellion, isolation, and self-reliance, as well as gender-identity confusion, were all present at my birth. They laid the groundwork for decades of all sorts of colorful adventures. Always on the go, I was like the Energizer Bunny, endlessly beating my own drum, dashing from one place to another, dancing with high-flying and underground-scurrying creatures. My curiosity took me to dangerous places as I hungrily sought out new adventures. If I ever had a stop button, it never worked. Born without an instruction manual on how to live life, I probably would not have used it even if I had one. Following rules was not my forte.

## Beating the "I Don't Want to" Drum of Rebellion

There are people on this planet who naturally follow directions, instructions, orders, manuals, rules, and laws. I salute you and offer my apologies if my unruly or rebellious tendencies have ever perplexed you or wreaked havoc in your life or on your sense of well-being. The good news is that I now understand and appreciate how the Universe pairs us together. You and I form beautiful crystalline structures, like snowflakes.

The Universal Law of Polarity is at work here. Where there is light, there is dark. Light is beautiful because of darkness, and darkness is stunning with glimmers of light. Cold brings relief to heat, as heat brings relief to cold. Goodness transforms evil, as evil challenges goodness to shine.

You might like *occasional* spurts of spontaneity in your life, whereas I thrive on change and surprises. Show me the framework or structure you are working within, and I can stream creative yet functional ideas that spark life into your systems. Let our coexistence integrate the combination of steady balance and flowing energy to whatever needs our special touch. We may seem very different on the outside—like the parts of a tree—but as great collaborators, we can strengthen the network of energy that makes good things happen!

This reminds me of the crew of Starfleet officers on the USS *Enterprise* (NCC-1701) from the original *Star Trek* television series. Despite having significantly different personalities, they executed successful missions and brought greater peace and harmony to all galaxies. I cannot imagine what Captain Kirk, the charismatic, starry-eyed, and visionary leader, would have done without First Officer Spock, the inexhaustibly logical pillar of reason. Together, they formed a dynamic duo and were able to accomplish more than what each could have done on his own. In my eyes, they truly honored and exemplified the principles of "we" and "unity." ○8

## Beating the "Leave Me Alone" Drum of Isolation

There are people on this planet who love to socialize with others, to manage multiple conversations simultaneously, and to engage fully in their loved ones' lives. I salute you and offer my apologies if my self-isolating tendencies have made me appear to be indifferent to your generosity. Thank you for sharing your adventurous spirit and excitement for life.

The good news is that I now appreciate our flourishing together. Embracing community is much easier than surviving alone. My conscious awareness of the Universal Law of Oneness propels vibrant energy within and around me. In my eyes, Einstein was correct in saying that it is only an illusion that we are separate beings; each one of us is part of a greater entity. The stars across the velvet-black sky may appear to be separate but are part of one Universe. You and I are connected to the stars, and the stars are connected to us. Our past, present, and future selves are all part of "one," as well.

Facing our illnesses, compulsions, and addictions together makes sense; suffering alone does not. The Universe has shown me that individuals who keep to themselves spend their final days on this planet brokenhearted, angry, and lonely. Hiding secrets and burying their talents, they often lose hope for good health, stable and loving relationships, and financial security. I have met and buried too many of them.

Blessed are those who allow themselves to experience unity in overcoming adversity—far more effective than self-isolation. Like animals in the wild that keep within their herd, flock, or den, we gain strength in numbers. Healthy companionships produce a higher quality of life for all. By staying connected with one another, we stimulate energy flow through our bodies at the cellular level and decorate our planet with infinite strings of holiday lights. How vibrantly we glow together!

## Beating the "I'll Do It Myself!" Drum of Self-Reliance

There are people on this planet who love and care deeply for others. Wholeheartedly offering their compassion, time, and energy, they sincerely reach out to help even those who deny needing assistance. I salute you and offer my apologies if my attitude of self-reliance has ever blocked you from the joy of giving or supporting me. If my stubbornness has exacerbated your anxiety over my safety and well-being, understand that I was protecting myself with a shield that served me well for a long time. I did not know how to begin to let it go.

Being tough and working hard was what I valued highly for most of my life. However, my self-reliance blocked me from many blessings. The good news is that with my understanding of the Universal Law of Allowing (granting ourselves and others permission to be in our own power, which allows good things to flow into our lives), I now open doors to receiving strength from an all-knowing and always-generous source of power. Today, I accept people's help and being showered with joy and comfort. I live my life in harmony while allowing others to live their lives. This gives blossom to kind thoughts, words, deeds, and love— great energy that flows freely throughout my body and into all areas of my life.

When resisting ideas and help from others before, I wasted a lot of time and energy with the "I'll show you!" attitude and struggled alone just to prove that I did not need anything from anyone. This fed my ego but kept my gas tank empty. Early AA folks referred to persons like me as an "intellectually self-sufficient man or woman" who believed that "[i]ntellect could conquer nature." (*Twelve Steps and Twelve Traditions of Alcoholics Anonymous*, the AA "12x12," page 29). Relying upon my brainpower alone was what I knew best. My entire identity was "the evangelical atheist."

You see, I was the little girl in the sandbox at the playground who told all the other children, "Your parents are lying to you. There is no such thing as Santa Claus or the Easter Bunny. And there is no such thing as God!" As you can imagine, my parents received numerous phone calls from unhappy parents. But that did not stop me. My little body housed a tanker of conviction and job satisfaction. As I grew older, I appealed to my schoolmates' logical side with "Look, scientists have discovered that we use only 10 percent of our brains, which leaves 90 percent unaccounted for. This 'God performing wondrous acts' idea is really the work of that 90 percent of our brains. Just use all of your brain, and you'll be fine. There is no God." Quite the charmer I was—not. When friends shook their heads and said nothing, I rejoiced in thinking, "I am right, *again!*" Ო

Nothing less than a miracle could have changed my mind about the non-existence of God. Some folks believed I needed a brick to land on my head to wake up. That did happen—a spiritual brick and countless inexplicable, non-tangible experiences my conscious brain could not comprehend. I had been an evangelical atheist for decades, but it was a series of strange events that transformed me and guided my decision to be baptized Catholic in my mid-thirties. This might be a wonderful subject for another book. I realize that being Catholic is not for everyone, but in my opinion I wear it well. Saint Francis of Assisi will always be my humble hero—probably because Jesus was also *his* humble hero. Moreover, Blessed Mother Mary has done an outstanding job in guiding me gently to fill my everyday life with compassion for myself and other living beings. For this I will be forever deeply grateful.

## Deliberate Recovery Works

Allowing the sunlight of the Spirit to guide me through my days and nights, I am able to make decisions easily and with greater confidence than in the past. Despite CRPS and a myriad of health complications, I truly enjoy the presence of a divine source of unlimited strength and wisdom. Imagine that. Not relying on the brain between my ears has created smoother paths for me. How I used to stumble around in the dark hoping to avoid running into walls and furniture, while the light switch had been there all along. I was the one who refused to turn it on. Doing things the hard way was my way. Thank goodness, another atheist bites the dust.

Wait a minute. You might want to sit down for this. Today, I also do not mind being wrong and will admit it the very second I realize it. If you show me where my mistakes are, I immediately find gratitude in seeing what is right or correct. My hunger for truth and clarity overrides my lust for denial, numbness, and vagueness. Needing to be right about everything no longer interests me. How do you like them apples? I no longer "drink poison and wait for the other person to die" (as we say in 12-step recovery), and gone is my knack for ruining good things and sabotaging myself. Now I am free to pursue dreams I never felt I had the right to wish for or want.

You, too, can choose this freedom of feeling fantastic in your body and dreaming big on this planet by first dismantling the resentment-making, self-blaming machine between your two ears. Adopt the *26 Self-Care Vigilante Affirmations* and watch the false beliefs about yourself lose their power over you, as mine have. It does not happen overnight, but little by little, you will find something to be grateful for even when you are wrong about a situation or a person. Freedom from distorted perceptions of the truth helps us celebrate anything and everything, including mistakes that can produce many wonderful results. ଔ

Deliberate recovery works. Continuously nourishing our mind, body, and spirit with guidance from the Universe keeps us and the general public safe. We need not pile unnecessary angst and burden upon our backs and waistlines. If you in some way believe that misery is what you deserve, you will attract more of it and push away happiness. However, if you desire something different, then move and circulate the energy within you so that changes can happen around you. Become more aware of how the Universal Law of Attraction and Repulsion works in your life. Embrace the simultaneous presence of contrasting elements, such as light and dark (Universal Law of Polarity) and choose carefully the people in your inner and outer circles, as "like energy" attracts its own kind (Universal Law of Proximity). Get clear on the kind of person you were born to become and live in that creative energy *with integrity*. Own it.

My learning to recognize and pursue whatever I need to function well has been immensely valuable. While doing so, I embrace the presence of opposites, move energy within me to release what has been stuck, and invite whatever strengthens my mind-body-spirit connection with the Universe. My letting go of the energy of anger, sadness, guilt, shame, embarrassment, and disappointment has uncovered an abundance of so many favorable options and opportunities that surpass my expectations.

Feeling satiated—full and satisfied—is a wonderful state of being, with or without material gains. Understanding the Universal Law of Sufficiency and Abundance has served me very well. Having experienced so many different types of craving and longings (not feeling full and satisfied) gave me newfound appreciation for the existence of plenty. I no longer need lots of alcohol, food, money, work, sex, and everything else under the sun to make me happy. Everything I truly need and appreciate is already *within* me. I have been carrying those passions and planted visions that the Universe instilled in me long ago. And now I am bringing them to life! Nourishing myself and nurturing my surroundings, I emerge into the world as the creative being I was intended to be all along (Law of Emergence, as explained by Derek Rydall). May you choose the creative life you were meant to live, as well. ☙

Thank you for allowing me to take you on this trip back to the delivery room of the hospital where I was born. You now know that I lived a significant part of my life madly driven by these mantras: "I don't want to," "Leave me alone," and "I'll do it myself!" Confession: there still is a small part of me that thinks being defiant is sexy. Fortunately for all of us, I have flushed much of that conflicting energy from my system at the cellular level. Slowly but steadily the defiance in me has dissipated through the process of neutralizing reversed or scrambled energy created by physical injuries, trapped emotions, an overextended sense of responsibility for others, excessive adrenaline and cortisol, environmental chemicals and metals, and other toxins. From groaning to glowing, I am truly grateful to feel so fantastic.

With a light-filled heart and a full tank, I now have so much more to offer people in ways I had never imagined possible. My ability to give and accept help from others with grace and gratitude— rather than grinding my teeth and grimacing in exhaustion—has become one of the key ingredients of my spiritual growth and happiness on Earth (Universal Law of Giving and Receiving). Being fully present while serving others, I allow the daily flow of love and blessings from the Universe to connect me more deeply with people and Mother Nature. Can it get any better than that? Yes, it certainly can (Universal Law of Increase). Just keep reading! ಜ

## Exercise for Chapter Two

*Ilana's Mindfulness Meditation and Tapping Exercise for NEW THOUGHTS AND HABITS in a 5-Part Format (adapted Progressive Energy Field Tapping or Pro EFT\*)*

Below are passages you may reflect on as you breathe deeply (CS) in silent meditation or say the words aloud while relaxing and tapping together the SIDES of both palms of your hands—the "karate chop point" (KC Point). (*See APPENDIX A: Tapping Meridian Points.*) For tappers, you may refer to APPENDIX B: Expanded Version of Chapter One's exercise, for guidance.

REMEMBER: Please drink some water before, during, and after this exercise. This is a vital part of cleansing and refreshing your body.

❖ Reversal 1: "Even though my working hard to do the right thing for everyone else leaves me tired, frustrated, and repeatedly making mistakes, there's a part of me that doesn't want to let it go and deprives me of feeling refreshed and positive about my accomplishments for some reason—known or unknown, logical or illogical. But I want to love and accept myself anyway." CS

❖ Reversal 2: "Even though my wanting to be right all the time about my beliefs, opinions, and behavior hurts my relationships with others and keeps me from freely relaxing and laughing around people, there's a part of me that doesn't want to let it go, for whatever reason. (Maybe I have to prove that I'm valuable and indispensible, or I really need to be heard, acknowledged, and admired.) But I want to love and accept myself anyway." ❧

❖ Reversal 3: "Even though the part of me that always wants to be right and to stick to my old ways still keeps me stuck on the hamster wheel, I want to start letting go of thoughts, words, and actions that drain me, because I love and accept myself." ❧

❖ Reversal 4: "Even though this remaining desire to do things my way—and what I think is best for everyone else—complicates my health, schedule, and wallet, I choose to trade in my old thoughts and habits to live a life full of grace, ease, and laughter. And I love and accept myself deeply and completely." ❧

❖ CHOICE Statement: "I choose to give myself permission to breathe freely, move forward, and create a life beyond anything I could imagine on my own. Thank you, Universe, for your mercy, hope, and strength. Continue to show me that I am worth it! And I deeply and completely love and accept myself." ❧

*\*Pro EFT™ (Progressive Energy Field Tapping™)*
*and the process of reversal neutralization or "Reversal*
*Setup" were developed by EFT Master Lindsay Kenny.*

# CHAPTER THREE

# Roots of Constipation

## Fog and Denial

From where I sit, constipation stinks. Allow me to explain without getting too graphic. When my internal plumbing was not working very well, I felt heavy and bloated. Any effort to think clearly was downright exhausting. I became extremely irritable whenever unable to recall something I should have remembered. When my bowels were constipated, I was emotionally stuck as well. And whether or not medical journals acknowledge the term *mental constipation*, I had it. My brain hurt without headaches. At that point, my vocabulary contained barely two words: "Blah" and "Crap." This is the Parental Guidance (PG) suggested version, of course.

Today, I have no doubt that my physical discomfort, lack of mental clarity, and emotional disturbance were all connected. For example, my head was fuzzy and my intestines were clogged when I ate bread, pasta, cheese, and some other foods. Then my sinuses became inflamed, and the pressure in my face was unbearable. Stuffy head, mental clutter, and abdominal constipation produced a very grumpy, moody person. Ice cream, syrup, and chocolate ignited blissful sugar highs but cheated me out of the many benefits of deep, restorative sleep and a robust immune system. Blah!

Not getting enough deep sleep, I wasted a lot of time and energy trying to accomplish simple tasks and backtracking to correct mistakes made from haste and brain fog. Low productivity and procrastination plagued me like skunk perfume, which is practically unshakable and really, really stinks. Combine all that with my compulsive mental masturbation: circular, repetitive thinking that stole precious time and kept me from living in the present moment. Regurgitating the past and forecasting the future consumed me as I engaged less and less with the world. Too exhausted to change my personal habits, I could only hide in pain and relentless brain fog, insomnia, and constipation. Denial kept me running hard and going nowhere fast on my hamster wheel of disappointment, frustration, and shame.

Depression blocked my ability to feel grateful. When believing that people were untrustworthy, unreliable, and unloving, I naturally attracted more of exactly that into my life. I looked for and found evidence that this world was an unsafe place and insisted that I was right about this. Blind to my resentful and unforgiving attitudes, I created more of what was familiar to me—a world filled with criticism, judgment, and doubt. Gratitude was not part of this equation. Reflecting upon my years of struggle, I can see clearly that appreciation (gratitude) and punishment (resentment) can never occupy one's mind at the very same time. Your reading this book right now means that I have chosen to fill my mind with appreciation for anything, one day at a time and many days in a row, and am now sharing this gratitude. ♋

## Not-So-Yummy Depression

I do not recall exactly when, but at some point during the past eight-and-a-half years, the Universe gave me special lenses through which I gained the ability to spot people on this planet who do not really want to be here. In their bodies and on Earth, they do not feel safe. What they see around them disgusts them: intolerable unfairness and corruption everywhere. People they love go away while destructive ones stay. They are frustrated watching their limbs go weak, suffering while sleeping, and struggling in a body that fails them. Many are watching the clock and just biding time until their departure. Their disappointment runs deep in their exhaustion and hunger for the pain to stop. Experiences in their bodies have not matched their expectations. Focused on what is broken or what they lack, they refuse to see and celebrate the good within themselves and their lives. These are the walking dead; they appear to be alive, but somewhere deep within, they aspire to disappear.

Occasionally, a few glimpses of gentle light and hope awaken them. They reach and grab onto something to love and cherish, sometimes daring to believe that they can have one day without disappointment or pain. But suddenly, they retreat quickly into hiding and darkness again, because they find the light too bright, love so fleeting, and hope merely momentary. Still surviving, they detach from their bodies to some degree and fantasize about no longer being here.

So, at airport bars they wait, watch, and wonder. Between the sheets they wait, watch, and wonder. In hospital beds they wait, watch, and wonder. In wheelchairs and walkers they wait, watch, and wonder. Under blankets and boxes they wait, watch, and wonder. On couches in the dark, they wait, watch, and wonder. Many wait, watch, and wonder with their hands on cookies, chips, cigarettes, alcohol, joysticks, weed, blow, money, cards, guns, porn, somebody else's husband or wife, someone whose name they do not even know, or on a steering wheel heading out of town with hopes of finding greener grass. Perhaps, they may one day feel alright to be alive. ❧

I see these people clearly. The Universe brings me everything that is already somehow a part of me or within me. "You spot it; you got it!" is an expression that speaks volumes. We all serve as mirrors for one another. Even during moments of denial that I was depressed, I must have been very much not well at all, thank you, as miserable people kept popping up before me—in stores, restaurants, on TV and movies, in gas stations, you name it. Undoubtedly, a continuous thread of energy links us all together. A connection exists even when we might prefer it not to be there.

My personal darkness was dastardly but necessary. There was no single method, approach, modality, tool, program, system, religion, or pill that brought me out of depression. I reached for anyone and anything that the Universe deemed necessary for my recovery journey, which included setbacks, progress, and even more setbacks to moving forward again. Everything was valuable: experienced doctors, inexperienced doctors, religious folks, non-religious folks, seasoned therapists, bright-eyed therapists, happy people in 12-step recovery, miserable people in 12-step recovery, enlightened psychiatrists, and perplexed psychiatrists. You get the picture. ଔ

## Nowhere to Go but Up

With CRPS and my inability to think clearly, I was completely unaware that the electrical system in my brain was short-circuiting with high frequency and duration. My neurosynaptic response went haywire. My transmitters fired signals, but I was "out to lunch," like when sent email messages get lost in cyberspace and never arrive. Or in baseball terms, my brain was getting ground balls to shortstop, but with no one there to cover second base, I kept missing what should have been easy double plays. *ARGH!*

Despite a solid education, extensive experience in both the public and private sectors, and numerous accomplishments in blue, pink, and white-collar industries, I was stumped. No amount of money could erase my pain, and all the education and technology in the world could not give me back my intelligence. How fortunate I was that the spirits of my ancestors appeared to me when I was in tremendous physical agony. Even though they were part of the Universe I could not see, their presence was strong in guiding me to find people who were ready and able to help sort through mountains of information about remedies that could potentially bring me relief.

Prescription pain medications, physical therapy, and other modalities to reverse muscle atrophy and control pain do work for many people. But putting this body of mine back together again required a full commitment from all parts of me to collaborate in my restoration or healing process. Nothing less than having every cell in my body wanting the same thing would have worked. Great quarterbacking is crucial, but it takes an entire team to win a Super Bowl.

Even though I have always loved team sports, remember one thing: I was born a contrarian. Not following rules, orders, instructions, and guidance was my modus operandi for most of my life, because I was always an exception to the norm. Most people burned their hands when they touched a hot stove, but that did not apply to me. Most people gained weight from eating tubs of ice cream, but I believed ice cream had no calories in my body. Most people's motor skills were badly affected by alcohol, but I was a much better driver under the influence. In the world according to me, alcohol was highly instrumental in improving my motor skills and dexterity.

*Terminal uniqueness*, a phrase commonly used in 12-step recovery, perfectly described my state of mind. I excelled at denying my unhealthy condition and negative patterns of behavior. Many of us, even when at death's door, still cling to the belief that we are uniquely different from other people with problems and would not benefit from anyone's guidance. "I'm not like you, and I can prove it—you'll see. Now go away!" is our unspoken mantra. All of my distorted perceptions of reality polluted my brain and granted me permission to contaminate my body. The more I contaminated my body, the more polluted my thinking became. Can you say "hamster wheel," anyone? ❄

Once upon a time, I believed that other people should listen to their doctors and pharmacists about medications. My preference was to be my own doctor and pharmacist, deciding what, when, and how much I should be taking. Most people would benefit from sleeping and eating regularly, but I was under the impression that I could cruise smoothly without having to waste time on sleep, rest, and all that other stuff. When I learned that Benjamin Franklin was not a fan of sleep, he instantly became one of my childhood heroes. Cookie Monster, of the educational television show *Sesame Street*, was another role model of mine—well into my adulthood. "Cookieeee!?! Yum, yum, yum!!!"

In hindsight I think it was very possible that, since birth, I had been physically or at least energetically constipated in countless ways. Born severely anemic and colicky, I absolutely refused to be breast- or bottle-fed. Perhaps when I arrived on Earth, I had changed my mind about wanting to be here. I refused nourishment from my mother, the nursing bottle, and everything else. Having received blood transfusions through my forehead and other procedures during my infancy, I was forced to stay alive. Even though my health stabilized, there was a rebellious part within me that furiously asked, "Whose idea was it to put me in this female body anyway?" My actions retorted, "Never mind. I will do whatever I want with it!" And *that*, I did.

Eastern wisdom and practices showed me how to take the leap I needed for all parts of me to be on the same page, including my grandstanding defiance and rebelliousness. The most significant lesson for me during the early stages of my physical recovery was that I must embrace the pain and all my disabled body parts, rather than emotionally abandon them. Instead of writing off my foot as "dead," I learned to treat this hypersensitive, blackened part of me like a precious newborn infant. From somewhere inside me emerged a delightful little song. I began to sing to my foot with much tenderness and excitement for its arrival and survival. How beautifully it responded to this expression of love!

Applying this mindset and powerful energy toward other parts of my body and internal organs, I gained a mind-body-spirit connection that cleared so many pathways both within and around me. My gut intuition became sharper and stronger, filled with my Creator's courage, wisdom, and energy. **And today, whenever obstacles come my way, I immediately expand my breath, spirit, and consciousness, trusting that the Universe can and will lift me above them and propel me forward in living my purpose on this planet.** This trust has become my new definition of serenity. That power is always there for me, especially when I ask, believe, and receive. ❧

## Hope for My Butt and Body

Pain is powerful. My many gifts of desperation taught me how to find and enjoy the freedom I have now. They continue to promise me even higher levels of freedom that the brain between my ears has yet to comprehend. Truly believing that "pain is a touchstone for spiritual growth" (from *Alcoholics Anonymous: The Story of How Many Thousands of Men and Women Have Recovered from Alcoholism*, the "Big Book," page 63), I have great hope for the rehabilitation of my butt, body, and brain through a divine guidance that has and will continue to deliver many more wonderful and delicious experiences to come.

Before all of this I was never a fan of pain— except for a period of time when I announced to the world that pain was pleasure. Lying to myself about this and many other things, I fiercely sought quick fixes for my discomfort that made everything worse. Short-term solutions for immediate gratification compounded my physical, mental, and emotional constipation.

**To get out of this vicious cycle, I had to admit that treating the mind, body, and spirit simultaneously was the strategy I had missed adopting all along.** Simply, a three-legged table needs all three legs. Feeling good in my body required 1) a continuous re-commitment to retraining they way I perceived myself and the world, 2) safe methods for resolving the multitude of traffic jams in my internal organs and systems, and 3) the rebuilding of my body's structure through ongoing communication with my Creator by using my gut intuition and spiritual umbilical cord to the Universe. Finding relief and comfort required all of these integrated and interdependent projects. The principles of honesty, humility, willingness, and open-mindedness were all essential for resolving the pain in my buttocks—literally *and* figuratively. ☙

I discovered that when my butt is happy, I am happy. If my butt is disgruntled, watch out! Human buttocks contain six sets of large muscles, and two of mine became drama queens. When my obturator and piriformis muscles screamed for help, the intensity of pain drastically interfered with my ability to make appropriate decisions for a better quality of life. With racing thoughts and foggy brain, I froze and forgot to eat, or ate too much, breathed shallowly, and could not take good care of myself. In surrender mode, I acquired patience and healing time and learned ways to develop good, long-lasting, healthy habits, such as re-adjusting my posture for better musculoskeletal structure, expanding interior space for my organs to function more efficiently, stretching out deep layers of muscle for greater blood flow, drinking warm-to-hot water to flush out bodily waste, and many more fantastic habits that inspired my *26 Self-Care Vigilante Affirmations.*

My butt pain is not a world crisis. Yes, it is. No, it isn't. Well maybe. Having discomfort in this particular area definitely adds to one's emotional distress. This is true not only in my case. During an "a-ha" moment I realized that unhappy "deep-six" muscles keep many of us from sitting comfortably, thinking clearly, and functioning smoothly. Note that this discussion extends much further than my rear end—or yours. Suffering from tight, agitated, or weakened buttock muscles, leaders throughout history could have made decisions that negatively impacted the world. I need not list names, but you get the picture.

People in positions of influence must pay close attention to this entire region on a regular basis. I am officially declaring that their list of duties should include butt care. Executives, legislators, judges, researchers, and business and world leaders who sit for long hours in airplanes, laboratories, offices, and conference rooms are at high risk of making

unfavorable decisions. This world and future generations may benefit from our leaders sitting for
shorter periods of time; stretching their hips, butts,
and legs throughout the day; and finding ways
to gain relief from their constipation and bladder
issues. Right at this moment, dare to imagine a more
peaceful world filled with happy tailbones and
tushes. What a dream! ☙

Letting peace begin with me, I searched int-
en-sely and reached out to others for solutions that
might relieve me of physical pain and emotional
constipation. Nothing less than a diverse combination of tools helped me, some of which included
physical therapy, aqua (pool) therapy, neuromuscular therapy, 12-step recovery, psychotherapy,
craniosacral therapy, Chi Gong (the Chinese art of
energy movement), Emotional Freedom Technique
(EFT) and Progressive Energy Field Tapping (Pro
EFT™), and mindfulness meditation. They empowered me to strengthen the flow of energy within
my body and beyond the walls of my skin. While
working with nutritionists, energy workers, personal trainers, and other specialists, I began taking
responsibility for what I put into my body. My
physical fitness required mental fitness as well.
Both the thoughts I kept out of my mind and those
I welcomed truly made a significant difference in
my health and overall quality of life.

Combining knowledge of kinesiology (muscle
testing) with nutrition gave me greater understanding of how to make my internal organs, glands,

and systems feel happy again. In response to what my body was telling me, I identified which foods, pathogens, and environmental toxins irritated me. To the best of my ability, I gradually began eliminating them from my meals, soaps and shampoos, cleaning products, and other items in my home.

You too can begin finding out which foods irritate and make you weak by getting an allergy test (which tests for allergies to over a hundred foods and environmental allergens) at a traditional Western Medical clinic and a naturopathic assessment to detect possible sensitivities to foods and environmental contaminants. Tune in to your internal organs. When they feel heavy, tired, or constipated, begin avoiding the irritating foods, air, or other things that could be contributing to or intensifying the inflammation (swelling) in your digestive system. Start giving your small and large intestines much needed rest by staying away from what you are allergic or sensitive to. Then investigate further what, when, and how much your body truly needs. I encourage you to find strong support from good listeners and people who have been through this journey as well. This can be a very rewarding experience for everyone participating.

I took full responsibility for my past unhealthy behaviors, including putting into my body the foods and other substances that kept my organs and systems from healing and functioning optimally. Owning those behaviors and overcoming my subconscious resistance to change, I eventually embraced habits that put an end to self-sabotage and self-annihilation. The right foods allowed me to do the exercises with neuromuscular-skeletal therapists and rehabilitation trainers that reversed my muscle atrophy (deterioration) and rebuilt my stabilizer muscles. Gradually, I regained higher levels of functioning: greater range of motion, strength, and stamina. The hard work was painful but also granted me relief from pain. The art of knowing when to push versus when to relax and heal is delicate. Take time to develop this skill. My body spoke, and I stayed quiet enough to listen. Simple. Not easy, but simple.

To this day I still agree with people who say, "Physical fitness begins in the kitchen." When we eat nourishing foods, our bodies perform better. On the other hand, "garbage in; garbage out." When I feel like crap, I eat crap; when I eat crap, I feel like crap. Oh that hamster wheel again! On that note, I daresay that kitchen fitness begins in our small intestines. Our small intestines are the real brains, for they determine what our bodies need to absorb versus what they should eliminate. The brain between our ears can lie to us. Reliance upon our gut intuition regarding what to eat helps to nourish us and produce sufficient energy to perform at higher levels.

Remember this: what may *look like* food might not be real food that our bodies can convert into vibrant energy. Keeping our mitochondria (structures within the cells that convert oxygen and nutrients into energy) happy is pivotal to great health. The more I eat what is appropriate for my body, the higher my energy levels. Having less pain, fatigue, and brain fog sounds like a pretty good deal to me. One day at a time, I choose foods filled with nutrients over those that keep me dependent upon wheelchairs and walkers. ∝

## Freedom from Constipation

Hours, days, nights, weeks, months, and years of intense treatment and rest periods shaped my lifestyle, but it was all worth it. I became intimate with the blood flowing through my vessels and mindful of the oxygen–carbon dioxide exchange in the cells of my internal organs. The food-processing factory within my body (digestion) spoke to me loudly through my poop-making factory (elimination). My relationship with my skin became a celebration of amazing teamwork, for I read and honored its clues as to which internal organs or systems needed special attention (*viscero-cutaneous reflex*). Using my very own fingertips and gut intuition, I skillfully enhanced my body's natural flow (*cutaneo-visceral reflex*) by actively clearing any traffic congestion in my energy superhighway (meridian system). Releasing trapped energy has allowed my internal organs to heal, survive, and thrive.

Daily living has become a lot easier with my practicing the spiritual principle of open-mindedness. I consciously expand my mind's limited vision to access a splendid field of choices for rising above any obstacle. Either situation could be true: stuck energy in my body can create the perception of a roadblock, or my perception of a roadblock can manifest stuck energy. The combination of both is a vicious cycle. What I know is that physical, mental, emotional, and spiritual constipation is far from enjoyable. Therefore, my absolute favorite four-letter word that begins with the letter "F" is *"F.L.O.W.,"* which stands for *"Feel Light Offering Wisdom™."* I love feeling the light of my inner flame dancing within me and cherish the Light of my Creator upon the face of every one of my cells. Solutions are everywhere and can emerge now and every minute for as long as I remain open to them. My purpose on Earth is to encourage the natural flow of energy in everything to the best of my ability. And I let it begin within me.

I have witnessed the presence of an unlimited source of Power and Grace that resides in every cell of my body. Just as I feel God when I enjoy nature, I feel this Power and Grace within my body. Turning inward for a conscious contact with a higher power gave me great relief from spiritual constipation and the pleasure of no longer viewing my body as "damaged" or "abandoned." In the past I believed that someone had hit the wrong button when they sent my soul to Earth in a female body. Perhaps I could have been a Boston Red Sox catcher and captain, like Jason Varitek (same birthday, but five years apart), or a great designated hitter, like David Ortiz ("Big Papi"). However, with my new pair of lenses, glasses, or goggles, I am a team leader and homerun hitter in other ways.

Despite my old thoughts and challenges about being a guy in a chick's body, I have emerged as the complete and amazing being that I was always meant to be—with nothing missing, not even the bat and two balls that baby boys are born with. Finally admiring the body I have now—especially my vibrant internal organs—I no longer seek approval, love, or truth from the outside. Although evidence that I still feel like a guy in a chick's body pops up from time to time, all of my old anguish has melted away. What has surfaced is a great delight. I share more on this later and in Book 2 of this series. Stay tuned! ∝

The infinite source of information that has guided me in making wise decisions on a day-to-day basis has always been here for me. I feel comfortable in my own skin today, because I have finally acknowledged that divine perfection lives right here within me and in every single one of us. Today, how well I take care of my body, heart, and spirit demonstrates the depth of my appreciation and respect for my Creator. Day after day my recovery journey has proven to me that I have more options than I think. You do as well. Efforts to expose and flush any constipation or stuck energy in the mind, body, and spirit are meaningful to what is in our hearts and bodies on Earth and beyond. Real joy can be had when we remove what does not belong in us and replace it with the goodness we have deserved all along.

Remember that the Universe is immense, and we each have choices about which stars to reach for and include in our personal galaxies on earth. Embrace your power to see the world differently from how you viewed it in the past. When we stop staring at what is cold and heavy at the bottom of the ocean, we are better equipped to bathe in the timeless beauty of its dancing colors, silence, and sound. What an amazing choice this is! ☞

# Exercise for Chapter Three

*Ilana's Mindfulness Meditation and
Tapping Exercise for RELIEVING MENTAL
CONSTIPATION in a 5-Part Format (adapted
Progressive Energy Field Tapping or Pro EFT\*)*

Below are passages you may reflect on as you breathe
deeply (**CЗ**) in silent meditation or say the words aloud
while relaxing and tapping together the SIDES of both
palms of your hands—the "karate chop point" (KC
Point). (*See APPENDIX A: Tapping Meridian Points.*)

Please remember to drink some water before,
during, and after this exercise.

❖ Reversal 1: "Even though my repetitive negative
thoughts and feelings block me from enjoying
self-confidence, prosperity, and great opportunities right in front of me, there is a part of me that
doesn't want to let it go for whatever reason. I'm
stuck reliving the past and forecasting the future,
but I want to love and accept myself anyway."
**CЗ**

❖ Reversal 2: "Even though my mental consti-pa-
tion and 'stinking thinking' keep me sick, stuck,
and sad—blocking me from hope and visions for
a better future, there is a part of me that doesn't
want to let it go and wants to stay stuck. (Maybe
I learned this habit of thinking from someone or
need to take better care of my intestines.) There

is another part of me that wants to let it all go and flow. I love and accept both parts of me."
ଔ

❖ Reversal 3: "Even though all the tug-of-war battles in my head and tightness/fatigue/pain in my body still hold me hostage—preventing me from enjoying self-confidence, vibrancy, and love—there is a part of me that is ready to let go of my victimhood, and I want that part to win, because I love and accept myself deeply and completely." ଔ

❖ Reversal 4: "Even though this remaining residue of insecurity, hesitation, and constipation still weighs me down, I choose to let all of it go and take bite-sized steps in building a re-energized team of mind, body, and spirit. And I love and accept myself unconditionally." ଔ

❖ CHOICE Statement: "I choose to embrace all my strengths and weaknesses that prepare me to rise above boulders in my path and reclaim the amazing life I truly was born to have! And I deeply and completely love and accept myself unconditionally." ଔ

*\*Pro EFT™ (Progressive Energy Field Tapping™)*
*and the process of reversal neutralization or "Reversal*
*Setup" were developed by EFT Master Lindsay Kenny.*

# CHAPTER FOUR

# Immediate Gratification

## Expensive Pursuits

My name is Ilana, and I am addicted to immediate gratification. My lifelong mantra has been, "I want what I want *when* I want it, and I want it *now*—no ifs, ands, or buts!" Restless pursuit of anything that could instantaneously satisfy my cravings evolved into the monkey wrench that kept me from truly enjoying life on this planet. I spent years chasing moments of pleasure through food, alcohol, sex, work, and money, but ironically, all those highs led to lots of moans and groans from my internal organs to my wallet—especially my wallet. You heard it from me: sooner or later, unhappy organs lead to unhappy wallets. ✲

Underlying my desire for everything that could give me instant pleasure was my hunger for approval. I wanted evidence that people were glad that I had been born, that I was good enough and lovable in others' eyes, and that I was a valuable contributor to society. Workaholism, perfectionism, and the need to be right all the time were only symptoms of my true ailment. People, places, things, and substances gave me quick relief from pain caused by my perceived failures and my disappointments in self and society.

The problem was that quick fixes only temporarily helped me, but they produced heartache in the long run. I used people, places, and things to escape from the realities of being in my body, mind, and life. Wait, escape is too nice of a word. These so-called remedies helped me to abandon my body, mind, and life. They distracted me from actualizing and sharing the talents and gifts with which I was born. No, distracted is also too kind of a word. The quick fixes *divorced* me from a life that I was meant for—filled with grace, ease, and much laughter—like the one I have today.

My pursuit of instant gratification was extremely expensive. It cost me an incalculable amount of time, energy, and money and destroyed my self-confidence and many of my relationships. Joy that is readily available to all of us on this planet eluded me. Truthfully, I blocked this joy from myself. Too busy believing that my mind could solve everything, I worked long hours, ate and drank instant energy-boosting garbage, smoked all kinds of stuff, and sought validation from people whom I loved but could not rescue from drowning in their quagmire. In *my* blindness I could not see that my thoughts and actions were self-annihilating and disrespectful to the one who had created me. Whew! I am taking a deep breath right now. You may wish to do so too. ⊂⊃

My mind-body-spirit *disconnection* opened doors to insatiable cravings. Before the age of seven, I already was eating cherries—among other things—out of a gallon-size bowl. My parents did their best to monitor my portions, but I always found a way to put my tiny little fingers on more food than my tummy could handle. Never having patience to wait for goodies to cool down from the hot oven, I burned my mouth over and over again. "Lots of everything" was my rule-of-thumb. "Stop button" was not in my vocabulary. Of course I wanted other people to stop their nonsense, but never thought it would apply to me.

As an adult, my wanting more and more repeatedly pounded away any progress I made in inviting harmony. Within my very own skin and bones I was stuck listening to loud arguments between my head and heart. Condemnation from my mind to body and body to mind spawned incessant battles and left my soul desperate for nourishment. Certainly I had been aware of the existence of war among nations, economies, businesses, states, and families. But the wars between my two ears, my head and heart, hand and mouth, brain and wallet, and so on, were just as real and devastating.

What I did not know for almost four decades was that the electrical circuit within and around my body suffered ongoing disruptions. Shattered was the natural flow of energy that my body cells needed to grow and function optimally. Constipation in my bowels was chronic. And despite *learning* about healthier foods, I was not able to overcome my resistance to change. ○ℰ

## Drama Queen Extraordinaire

Knowing something helpful does not necessarily mean we take action to bring that goodness into our everyday lives. I had to become willing to let go of my resentments toward healthy habits before I could adopt them. The health and quality of my life now is proof that my efforts and the sincerity of everyone supporting me have made this long process so worthwhile.

Three-and-a-half years prior to my injury and CRPS, the world became a better, safer place after I put down the bottle and stopped drinking. This was at the tail end of 2003, after the New York Yankees eliminated the Red Sox in the bottom of the 11th inning of the 7th game of the American League Champion Series that year. I was so sick, heartbroken (again), and tired of losing to *them.* Plus everything else in my life was a mess. Something *had to* change—rather it was *I who* had to do so. Leaving my home, relationship, job, and city and moving to a new place did not solve my problems. Everywhere I went, there I was—very busy blaming everyone else for making my life impossible. Not only was yours truly a dissatisfied creature, she made a lot of people miserable. By some miracle, *something*—not the brain between my two ears—got me to a room full of sober alcoholics who each took personal responsibility for finding gratitude in everything. This was weird, but I stayed.

Newly sober, I was still the star of my own soap opera, titled *As the Ilana World Turns, Days of Ilana's Lives,* or *The Young and the Ilana. Ilana, The Restless* might have captured me best. God bless the old-timers who put up with my antics but taught me well. Learning and practicing the steps, traditions, and tools of recovery was not easy by any stretch of the imagination, but the sewage in my mind, heart, and intestines demanded that I change one thing: everything.

When I landed in a wheelchair in early 2007, this "change one thing: everything" concept saved my butt again. Who would'a thunk? Being bedridden gave me time for serious reflection. I did not ask for it, and my hyper mind, butt, and spirit found this jail time none too sexy. That had to change. No, once again it was *I who* needed to breathe and live differently. Twelve-step recovery guided me in using contrary action to reverse old habits to create new ones. For example, if you used to tie your right shoe before the left one, now tie your left one first before the right. Gradually applying this to many of my thinking habits, behavior, and situations worked.

In a wheelchair I found myself in the school of hard knocks again, but the Universe opened up huge new doors for me to walk through—seemingly endless opportunities to reflect upon my relationship with my body and my body's relationship with the entire Universe. During this period, I had more than plenty of "one-on-one time" with my Creator. I learned to cherish healthy habits and practice them over and over again to be able to hang onto them no matter what.

However, this was not an easy job. As mentioned before, I love masticating. Even the thought of chewing makes me happy. Alcohol made it possible for me to finish college and graduate school. Sex and chocolate were my reasons for living. Cigarettes helped me to think clearly. Spending money made me look and feel good. Moving from one place to another gave me hope for the future. Drama-filled relationships fed me pleasure, as I specialized in fixing people who had "no problems." Pot made me forget pain. Credit cards gave me status. Lust saved me from boredom. Exercising cancelled cake binges. My buddies and I were "birds of a feather" that flocked together to indulge in passions and pursuits that made us feel alive at the edge of death. How could I possibly live without them?! ∞

Was I able to see what I was doing to my body, self-esteem, wallet, relationships, and career? Did I even know that I was missing the benefits of having stability and consistency in my life? In hindsight, none of these thoughts existed in my field of vision. My fixation was thrill-seeking to defy all who broke promises and did not protect children. I made little time for really living *in* my body and cultivating my talents and gifts to serve the world. Fully in my *dis-ease*, my mind recorded a library of injustice and corruption I had witnessed. Boy, was I super busy!

Declaring war by abandoning my true self was far from wise and a very severe outcome of rebellious living—or perhaps I should call it *rebellious dying*. "You can't hurt me any more, because I've already given up on myself!" A part of me stopped hoping for a better life before I even owned it. My objects of addiction and pleasure promised to erase the disappointment in myself and pain in my world, but they were unsuccessful. A great soldier of the dark side's army, I kept looking for the next great fix that could help me escape from all of this. Alcohol, "cunning, baffling, and powerful" (from the "Big Book," page 58), was not my only drug. But it was my alcoholic thinking that sabotaged me long before I could spell "die alone." ◌

Now let's talk about ice cream. I spent most of my life fully demonstrating that I could defy the Law of Diminishing Returns. Many economics professors commonly use ice cream sundaes to explain this law. In economic theory, the law of diminishing returns proposes that if you give an ice cream lover a sundae—preferably made with vanilla and chocolate ice cream, topped with hot fudge, whipped cream, and nuts—this person will eat it with great pleasure. When you hand over another one, you will be making the ice cream lover even happier.

Suppose you offer more and more sundaes, like eight or nine. Economists believe that the consumer would find less and less enjoyment with each sundae. Perhaps getting cold and experiencing "brain freeze" would not be fun, or his or her taste buds would get bored and stomachs would ache. For whatever reason, the ice cream lover would eventually hit a point at which he or she would slow down and stop. These economists have never met me.

I saw no point in stopping, even with a full stomach, frozen mouth, shivering teeth, stiff body, and empty container. More was better, and if you did not keep these sundaes coming, I would declare you an incompetent (impotent) waiter, grocery store clerk, partner, dope dealer, bartender, banker, or whatever. Enraged, I would see you as one who failed to supply me with the safety, sanity, and success I thought I was getting from ice cream, money, booze, and everything else. From my point of view, the Law of Diminishing Returns did not apply to me. I could not imagine ice cream to be anything but forever delicious. Always inspired to consume even more, I wore my badge of defiance with great pride. ❧

There it is. I was proud of my defiance. When people said that I would be better off without the targets of my affection or obsession, they were wrong. I aimed to prove that my self-sabotaging behaviors merited respect and awe. Ironically, giving up one target of affection or drug of choice helped to justify my indulgence in another. Fortunately, my insanity kept putting me on the train to other abstinence programs. To help me practice spiritual principles in all areas of my life, the Universe escorted me to numerous train stations. The truth was that I was too unsatisfied about so many things. My *dis-ease*—discomfort and outrage about being in this body—had manifested into so many symptoms and cravings. I had to find some way to manage them before they completely managed me. Ease, comfort, and happiness without fear sounded good, but they were all elusive until I realized that forgiving my ancestors for their imperfections would give me the chance for a happy life while blessing them at the same time.

## Emotional Hand-Me-Downs

Overwhelmed by my inability to manage all my extreme behaviors and interests, I found perceived comfort—pure insanity actually—in trying to make everyone else's lives as perfect as possible. This was the interesting twist to my excessive need for immediate gratification. Some thoughts were:

> *Whether or not I am comfortable, safe, and happy, I want you to be all right. Just tell me what you need, and I will do whatever it takes to give it to you and make sure you feel loved and valued during your stay on this planet.*

And "I will sacrifice and abandon myself so that you can have your heart's desire. That would make me happy." As if that was not enough, my subconscious thoughts went even further:

*To demonstrate my commitment to you, I will ignore my need to sleep well, breathe fresh air, and exercise, because I cannot rest until you're alright. Know that when we are not together, I will continue thinking about you and work hard to ensure your safety and security. There's no need for you to pay me rent for taking up space in my head. Save your money, because you need it more than I do. But rest assured, I will find a way to give you more money. Remember: When you're happy, I'm happy.* ✂

I inherited this thought pattern and behavior from my parents, their parents, and many previous generations. This self-abandonment culture is only one of the many hand-me-downs from my family's closet. Like the sweaters and coats that were too small or too large and never did fit me well, I respectfully wore them to continue my cultural traditions. Here was the problem: the pattern of abandoning myself for the sake of others did not grant me relief from chronic pain. Relief came when I turned inward and showered myself with love, respect, and care through my thoughts and actions.

According to my culture, I was being selfish. For many generations, they lived with pain and sorrow. However, had I not broken their cycle of violence against self, I would be behind bars, tied to a bed, or dead by now. Instead, I chose to seek the delicious warmth of sunlight upon my face and to reconcile with my body so that my visit on this planet would be what it was meant to be—both fruitful and fun!

Self-care and pain relief go hand-in-hand. Fulfilling my desire to better serve loved ones, my attention to detail in flushing out toxic energy, thoughts, and chemicals from my body became critical. I now promote public safety by not being a hazard on the road, around people, or anywhere else. My commitment to self-care has to outshine any hint of martyrdom and all its perceived merits. When the airplane cabin pressure drops, the yellow oxygen mask must go on the adult first in order to save the child. PERIOD. ✂

## Resentments and the Human Rat-Race

Like many people in modern civilization, I have become an instant-gratification junkie. Neuroscientists and psychologists often research and discuss the subject of immediate gratification. My fellow economists, sociologists, and policy analysts, as well, spend a great deal of effort and money in studying the pattern of consumer behavior as it relates to time. How we love our continuous supply of readily available coffee, remote controls, microwave ovens, magical weight-loss pills, pre-cooked foods, prescription medication, cell phones, and other electronic devices that keep us "connected" to the world, and so much more. These so-called "solutions" have paved the way for the development of even more advanced technology, not only in government and military research and high-tech industries but in farming, food manufacturing, medicine, and many others as well. Lavished with advanced technology and science, we prefer not to wait for anything. Members of the human rat race continue to voice their preferences by pouring money and time into getting their hands on and eating up these "right now" products and services. When we add the costs of medical treatment, rehabilitation facilities, and prisons to the mix, we have a more accurate picture of what that hamster wheel truly looks like. ❦

I own my part in cultivating my brain's neurological demand for satisfaction. In the past I believed that getting something immediately was always better than waiting for it. Feeling justified in seeking instant pleasure, I missed the rewards of being patient. This was a vicious cycle. My quick response to "your demands" reinforced my expectation of receiving an immediate response from you as well. We both deserved the A.S.A.P treatment. Anything different would be unreasonable, and anything less would breed resentment. There it is: immediate gratification brews expectations— *premeditated resentments.*

When we are agitated and angry about the injustices done to us and to our loved ones, the lower vibrational frequencies in our internal organs make us sick. Whether or not we directly point a finger to blame a person, group of people, or institution, feeling that we are owed an apology can weigh us down and cause disruptions in our bodies' electrical systems. When that happens, our organs suffer. ☙

We become homeless within our own bodies when we try to disassociate from pain and ignore our internal needs. A strong mix of anger and stress can tax our stomach, intestines, liver, lungs, heart, and kidneys, among other organs. We must not ignore this. Experiencing anger is natural and human, but like in the oil filter of an engine, dirt accumulates and can shut down an entire system. In addition to anger and resentment, we often also feel disappointment, guilt, agitation, and impatience. Out from us come harsh words, impulsive reactions, and a whole host of unpleasant outcomes, like emotional and physical separation, isolation, homicide, suicide, or premature death. ☙

I do believe there is a relationship between the frequency of our daily demands for immediate gratification and the frequency of negative emotional flare-ups. Through the demand for speed come high expectations of performance and letdown, disappointment, and resentment. Uncontrollable rage, illness, chronic anxiety, substance abuse, self-battery—negative self-talk, neglect, or injury—and many other conditions show up and distract us from living well. Spoiled by the instant gratification that remote-control devices offer, I have become less tolerant of traffic on highways and local roads, for example. Give me a remote control to part the sea of red lights so that I do not have to sit in traffic. Better yet, "Beam me up, Scotty!" for I too deserve privileges like that of Captain Kirk and other space and time travelers. The resentment-making machine between my two ears was like a monster truck on a wet dirt road. In response to people who broke their promise to me or disappointed me in some way, I revved my engine, splashed some mud, and justifiably brooded in anger. One of my old habits was holding my breath while waiting for apologies to come, but they did not and probably never will. Fantasizing many ways of proving that I was correct in my thoughts, words, and actions, I wasted so much energy running in the same spot and going nowhere fast on my human hamster wheel. The vicious cycle of higher demands and expectations grew bigger, faster, and crazier. ଔ

Losing the ability to stand on my own two feet created such ugly thoughts and resentments I would never have imagined harboring. For over a year, I envied people who could walk—especially those who enjoyed exercising in my neighborhood when I had such a hard time even getting to my toilet. "Who gave them permission to enjoy my neighborhood?" What an outrage. "You don't even live here—I do!" The rage produced poison in my body without me taking in any. With these negative emotions, I flooded my system with excessive adrenaline and cortisol (among other hormones) that coursed through my body and then crashed from exhaustion and intensified physical pain. *ARGH!*

Detoxing my body from all this and replacing the stinking thinking to truly recover required much footwork: writing the prayer, as mentioned on page 552 in the "Big Book"; meditating upon the St. Francis prayer on page 99 in the AA "12 x 12"; tapping on key meridian points, especially the liver point (LP); drinking alkaline water to neutralize acid or electrolyte water to rehydrate my cells; and eating lots of calciferous vegetables, like cabbage, broccoli, and cauliflower, to make my intestines happy. In a nutshell, I seriously needed to flush out all that crap.

To my great surprise, I discovered how much relief from physical pain I could gain by letting go of resentments toward myself and others. Neutralizing disrupted energy and promoting correct directional flow throughout my body brought me to a place where I could enjoy laughing and smiling more, while continuing to fill my mind with great thoughts and my body with wonderful endorphins.

It is no wonder why we as a society have challenges with our bodies, mental concentration, sleep, performance, relationships, and finances. Going faster can get us stuck, and wanting things sooner can make us wait longer. Our lives are unmanageable when we allow the energy of anger, frustration, and stress to expand and distract us. Keeping life simple is not easy. However, we can start by looking where our feet are pointed and watching what our hands and eyeballs are doing. They speak volumes. Yes, distractions complicate. ❃

## My Anti-Adulthood Pledge

My high expectations yielded deep resentments, but my subconscious desire not to be an adult made things worse. During my early childhood I believed that all adults knew everything and were able to solve any problem. Also they were fully capable of protecting children from anything or anyone that could hurt them. Or so I thought. With these beliefs in my heart, I faced great disappointment from my high expectations, time after time. Eventually, my body began to develop, and I was sort of O.K. with the physical changes. However, actually becoming an adult was unacceptable. I did not want what "you" had. No thank you. Not fun.

I searched for and discovered evidence that I was not the only one who felt this way. In one of the original *Star Trek* episodes, there were terrifying—or more like *terrified*—creatures called "GRUPPS," a shortened version of "grown-ups." The only children left on a deserted planet deliberately hid themselves from Captain Kirk and his landing party. They feared GRUPPS, for they had witnessed that when children reached puberty, they turned into horrifying beasts. The maturation process thrust them into a state of insanity in which they became extremely dangerous to themselves and others.

For well over four decades of my life, I had harbored my underlying belief that adulthood was horrifying and unsafe. Ha! No wonder I never wanted to grow up! Thankfully, this well-hidden belief finally surfaced while I was tapping. Able to release this angst and stuck energy from my body, I reversed my subconscious resistance to "putting on my big girl pants." I began to perform many of my "adult responsibilities," like practicing self-care, scheduling regular medical appointments, returning phone calls, paying bills on time, investing for the future, and much, much more, with a real smile.

One of the most obvious health benefits of releasing this angst about adulthood was that I stopped grinding my teeth while sleeping. I now happily use them for chewing—you know, the masticating thing. Being an adult is not so bad after all, especially when I do the best I can with what I have at the moment and trust that the Universe will download information, energy, and courage to me so that I may do whatever it deems important at that time. Today, I allow myself to be amused by my youthful charm while I shine magnificently as an adult. Self-care truly pays well.

Where I used to doubt the merits of designing a healthy way of life, I now experience that it is very much worthwhile and exciting to do so. Taking action to elevate my emotional, physical, and spiritual health above mere survival mode reaps countless benefits, both today and in my future. Am I worth it? You betcha! ☙

## Safety in Connecting with the World

There are two sides to every coin—at least the last time I checked. My old defiance and resistance to adulthood was brutal, yet somehow funny and entertaining. However, the fear and anger beneath them propelled me to disengage from the world. Alienating myself from people gave me a false sense of security. From the outside I appeared to be fine and engaged well with people. But inside me were expanding chasms of separation, compartmentalization, disassociation, and isolation. I fantasized about existing only in my own world, living in a cabin in the mountains with no one else around. This was, I believed, my path to safety that would spare me from disappointment and disillusionment. Living alone in nature could protect me in ways human society could not.

Thank goodness those days are gone. With willingness to grow, expand, and show up in the world wherever the Universe needs me, I love engaging my mind with body while being guided by Spirit. In my old comfort zone I got annoyed, angry, and disappointed very quickly. The Universe transformed my resentment-making machine into a powerful gratitude-making machine. Acceptance that Yin and Yang (shadow and light) is everywhere—and both very valuable—dissolved my bitterness and opened my heart. I now revel in the existence of an amazing source of power that is undoubtedly capable of helping me change for the better—in spite of myself. Miracles do happen.

Today, I am grateful for my willingness to look inward. Exploring and embracing many treasures within me, I no longer keep them buried but bring them to light. Rather than thinking that I am stuck with this body, I choose to celebrate life in my splendid body. Having "kind thoughts, kind words, and kind deeds" means I not only treat other people well but also lovingly care for my liver, intestines, neck and back muscles, adrenal glands, hips, hands, feet, and everything else. ෬

When we take good care of ourselves physically, emotionally, and spiritually we reap the benefits of generating good vibrations. Red blood cells can swim freely instead of clustering from anger vibrations. I no longer need to get sick after bouts of anger, either from holding it in (imploding) or letting it out (exploding). My careful choice of words, in thoughts and speech, save me from brewing anger in my body and all the drama that accompanies it. Today, I mindfully support my blood cells in doing their job of delivering nutrients to other cells and transporting waste out of my body as efficiently and effectively as possible. You, too, can actively participate in your recovery by thanking your heart for all it has done for you and letting it thank you back. Envision the flow of your vibrant life force (blood) and listen for your body's messages.

This is a glimpse into my heaven on earth: vibrancy at the cellular level. Deliberate recovery works. Ignoring internal organs and systems does not. Today, I feel robust enough to face everything I disagree with and embrace all that feeds my spirit. At the cellular level I continuously release any resentment and feelings of anger, shame, guilt, remorse, or disappointment. Whether you choose to take deep breaths, pray, meditate, make amends, tap, exercise, or help someone today, my hope is that you will find some way (or combination of ways) to release negative emotions and free your cells from unnecessary stress. Let us focus on expanding our spirits and allow continuous streams of exuberance and life to flow through us. The Universe is within you, as it is within me. Yes, recovery truly is an inside job. ❃

# Exercise for Chapter Four

*Ilana's Mindfulness Meditation and Tapping Exercise for RELEASING TRAPPED FEAR in a 5-Part Format (adapted Progressive Energy Field Tapping or Pro EFT\*)*

Below are passages you may reflect on as you breathe deeply (**C8**) in silent meditation or say the words aloud while relaxing and tapping together the SIDES of both palms of your hands—the "karate chop point" (KC Point). *(See APPENDIX A: Tapping Meridian Points.)*

Please remember to drink some water before, during, and after this exercise.

❖ Reversal 1: "Even though my staying in unsafe places and relying on people I cannot trust prevents me from breathing freely and owning my own life, there is a part of me that doesn't want to let it go for whatever reason. (Maybe I'm afraid to rock the boat or appear to be disrespectful or disloyal.) But I want to love and accept myself anyway." **C8**

❖ Reversal 2: "Even though my failures to protect myself block me from feeling well-rested, re-energized, and secure, there still is a part of me that refuses to stop taking responsibility for everything and everyone. (Maybe it's my duty, job, or identity, and I would be a bad person if

I let go.) But I want to love, accept, and honor myself anyway." 03

❖ Reversal 3: "Even though my resistance to taking good care of myself still leaves me exhausted and unhealthy and prevents me from thriving with confidence, there is a small part of me that is ready to acknowledge the bounty of beautiful, positive experiences in my life each day. And I want to strengthen that part of me in the spirit of loving, accepting, and celebrating *all* parts of me." 03

❖ Reversal 4: "Even though this remaining fear, doubt, and lack of trust in myself and others prevents me from feeling safe in my body and precious on this planet, I choose to align myself with a Source of infinite wisdom, light, and mercy and to feel treasured and well-protected. I love and accept myself deeply and completely." 03

❖ CHOICE Statement: "I choose to allow my Creator's strength, love, and light to grant me rock-solid courage to thrive, one day at a time, while caring for my soul and those of my loved ones—when we are awake and as we sleep. And I deeply and completely love and accept myself." 03

*Pro EFT™ (Progressive Energy Field Tapping™) and the process of reversal neutralization or "Reversal Setup" were developed by EFT Master Lindsay Kenny.*

# CHAPTER FIVE

# The Magnificence of Chi (Qi)

## A Voice for My Body

The thought of adding more delicious activities to my daily life increases my appetite for being here on Earth. Loving and hope-filled thoughts, words, and movements I see, hear, and feel *all* relax my body. *AH!* These high-vibrational frequencies inspire my body to create new healthy cells and release whatever it no longer needs. Experiencing balance and flow within me (homeostasis) is absolutely yummy.

My moving forward with joy is a demonstration of my willingness to be a team player. Rather than commanding my body to perform and meet my demands, I now give it a voice to say what is on its mind and show gratitude for its wisdom. Chronic pain—with all its neurological dysfunction—produced so much wreckage in my body and my wallet. However, my body has brilliantly guided me out of the quagmire: flushing out excess adrenaline, cortisol, natural and lab-created chemicals, environmental toxins, viruses, and damaging bacteria.

Although this did not happen overnight, I acquired much experience in using different protocols, remedies, and modalities for managing pain and rebuilding my immune system. Every day I still learn new ones that may work for me and help others as well. Thank you, body, for telling me what you like and do not like. Keep talking, and I will continue to listen. ⌀

During countless hours of physical therapy and rehabilitation, I intimately monitored the effect of different combinations of foods, medications, and exercises on my nervous system. The strategy of introducing only one or two new changes at a time gave me answers as I observed their effects on my mental clarity, physical comfort, range of motion, and regularity in bowel movement, for example. I was careful not to bombard my nervous system, overwhelm my mind, or shock my intestines with the new medications, doses, exercises, foods, and treatment modalities. The slogan "easy does it" was incredibly helpful in keeping everything in perspective. More was not necessarily better, and faster did not promise desired results.

You could say that my dedication to examining my poop proved fruitful. Without going into great detail here—as a conversation with your doctor or nutritionist might be helpful to you—the color, shape, size, and texture of my bowel movements gave me clues about what kinds of support my internal organs needed. You, too, can learn a great deal about what your body likes or dislikes and the condition of your organs by the appearance of your bowel movements. I, along with many of my friends with chronic pain and life-threatening illnesses, can assure you that practicing preventative medicine is far more pleasant than experimenting with treatments for full-blown illnesses. So, if you think of me while doing your business in the bathroom, then I have done my job. Laugh while you are on the toilet, and I will have earned my wings.

The positive changes in my life have been so significant that I wrote a personal contract with myself: I must laugh to pee-point every single day. Already in the habit of appreciating the bright side of every situation (gratitude), my contract now mandated that I search for the funny side of everything, too. Standing over my toilet bowl and examining my poop may not sound thrilling, but maintaining good health is a priority. Dark brown/ black stool (excrement) may indicate unusual bleeding inside the body and alerts us to seek medical attention. On the other hand, celebrating a healthy bowel movement is fantastic; I send my poop off with a blessing and a "thank you" for the visit. Then waving with enthusiasm, I watch it swirl and float on its merry way to a new home!

The more I smile, giggle, and laugh, the greater the muscle stimulation and movement in my lower abdominal areas. Yes, I believe in massaging my intestines—don't you? Life is really good; I get to have fun laughing, give my abs a good workout, massage my internal organs, poop in grand style, and watch what I no longer need depart with a bit of fanfare. Being sober has its perks.

Today, I have astounding mental clarity and focus that rarely surfaced during the earlier years of my living with CRPS. Giving my body permission to speak openly has served me well, as I make decisions that lead to recovery in all areas of my life—not only short-term relief. My good fortune has become yours as well. The brain between my ears could take me only so far; had I not given my body a voice and found many of these solutions, my drunk butt would have rapidly become a burden to society. **Keeping my intestines happy and following my gut intuition has shifted me from functioning minimally in survival mode to living on purpose with passion and laughter.**

People I have not seen in a while comment that I look younger every time we meet. Perhaps it is because I am finally enjoying a real childhood of my own design in this adult body. Feeling loved, heard, and respected, my internal organs beam brightly and perform with enthusiasm. Despite occasional ups and downs, the good news is that my "down" periods are much shorter and less frequent than before. It is amazing to witness how flowing internal energy manifests great outcomes from the inside out, especially when I am back on the dance floor seeing my muscle memory come alive! Deliberate recovery has been so deeply rewarding.

## Releasing the Baggage

Allow me to refresh your memory that I was born with an intensely stubborn streak—highly uncooperative and temperamental—which sounded like this:

*I'm alright. I want to do things my way, which is probably better than yours. But if you get good results, congratulations! Just because it's working for you doesn't mean it will work for me. So leave me alone. I will do it my way. Don't look over my shoulder. Go away. I am just fine!*

Quick—someone give me a vomit bag. Thank you, God, Source, Universe, Great Spirit, and all the angels and saints for protecting me from myself and sparing the world from my self-destructive tendencies. Transforming my *stinking thinking* (force energy) into a mindset of gratitude, growth, and unity (power energy) was no easy feat. With great exasperation people used rant, "Why do you *always* have to be right?" My one-word answer was just "Because." More patient ones asked, "Would you rather be right, or would you rather be happy?" To them I replied, "Both. Being right really makes me happy." *DUH.*

As energy within my body stirred and flowed more freely, I began to experience a significant shift. Gifts of wisdom from my ancestors and my faithful friends in 12-step recovery had saved me from a life of isolation and tunnel vision. Unexpectedly,

I learned to admit that I had been wrong about many things, including my perceptions of myself and of the world. It was not easy, but I let go of beliefs that were holding me back from truly living fully in my body and on this planet. Change on the inside ignited change all around me. However, for more than a year my body was unable to improve despite everything I tried. My legs looked and felt as if they would never be able to support my body again. Then, with one nice crash into a wall, I came alive once more.

## Magical Kiss for a Wall

One day as I rolled myself down the hall and into my living room, I accidently ran my wheelchair into a wall as though it had just suddenly appeared. The crazy part was that this wall had been right at that spot since 1937 when the house was built. Plus it was huge and obvious—not small or hidden. "Aw crap! Blah, blah, blah!" My mouth let out a long string of words that apparently had no care or shame, and I burst out laughing. It was not the words but rather the echoing of funny sounds flying from my tongue that almost made me pee in my pants. I then heard a voice in my head uttering, "Darn, I'm hilarious!"

It was the combination of joy and self-approval that propelled me forward in my physical recovery—not someone else's validation of me. The laughter I belted out spoke volumes. It was clear and sweet like bells made of Waterford crystal. From that moment on, I began to search for and find humor in almost everything in my everyday life—not just a little, but lots of it. This ringing laughter sparked something that had been asleep. The spirit world performed CPR on me and revived all the heartbeats within the gazillions of cells in my body.

Remembering this laughter produces vibrant surges of energy in me every time I think of it. Keeping the memory alive has helped me through many tough times. Making a mistake, like losing control of my wheelchair, is not so bitter but adds more fuel for laughter. Nowadays, I am very comfortable exposing my shortcomings and having a good laugh over them; this book is proof. Opportunities to correct my errors make life fun. I do not deliberately make mistakes, but they happen. Ergo, fun opportunities come my way, and I appreciate every unexpected gift of wisdom. ✑

Each and every day I have multiple opportunities to let go of emotions that make me feel heavy and limit my movement. Acknowledging, thanking, and dissolving sadness, anger, despair, and frustration within my body cells produces strangely peaceful results. For example, I now benefit from having let go of the hand-me-down baggage inherited from previous generations regarding sleep issues. For decades, I struggled with my reverse sleep/awake schedule, in which my body preferred beginning the day in the afternoon and going to bed just before sunrise. My mother, her siblings, and their parents and grandparents were night owls as well.

Resting well is so important for solid physical recovery, mental health stability, and maintaining a healthy wallet. I did love the freedom and tranquility of being a night owl, but having a strange body clock (Delayed Sleep Phase Disorder, a.k.a. DSPD) negatively impacted my relationships with people, finances, health, and many other aspects of my life. Although scientists have not identified a specific night-owl gene, there is much experiential evidence that members of my family perform at our peak—especially mentally—during traditional sleep hours. Despite all the changes in diet, alarm-clock settings, or work-rest patterns tried, we continue to function extraordinarily well after sun-down without the aid of caffeine, sugar, nicotine, amphetamine, or prescribed medication. You could say that we are far more genius at night than during the day.

Perhaps my family's reverse clock developed from decades of turbulent wartimes and sociopolitical unrest—when the darkness of night kept them safer, whereas the light of day was deadly. Or my ancestors witnessed tragedies that left emotional scars, weakening their eyes and contributing to their avoidance of daylight. Based on what I heard from them, my eyeballs probably would not have wanted to see clearly either. Deeply grateful am I to

have begun unlocking and unraveling the mysterious impact of trauma upon my genes and health.
As I face brutal truth, remain open-minded, and
demonstrate willingness to take action, the Universe
delivers results and carries me forward. ⋈

Having tried countless ways to change my body
clock (circadian rhythm), I gained positive results
after unearthing and releasing trauma my ancestors experienced. Eventually, I became ready to use
sleep modification tools and processes that had not
worked for me before. Today, I feel empowered to
embrace change in other areas of my life because
of my conscious efforts to release inherited multigenerational trauma and epigenetic predispositions
from my body's cellular memory. (Enjoy my "pizza
and calzone" analogy later in this book.)

I was not alone when I began to let go of the
heavy burden of sadness straining my body. The
Universe brought people into my life to accompany
me while I made efforts to stretch beyond my comfort zone. Without judgement, they guided me in
accepting and embracing my shadow side, while we
shared a mutual exchange of love and understanding. Together, we transformed the painful rocks in
our shoes into fine sand between our toes, as we
walked side by side on the beach of life. ⋈

The image of converting rocks into sand was
essential to my transformation. Energy broke stones
into smaller pebbles and produced fine-grain sand.
Whether or not we acknowledge it, we all do have

this power within us. Feeling fantastic in our bodies depends upon our commitment to keeping life-force energy—both in and around us—alive and flowing. For so many years I had forgotten about my ancestors' high regard for Chi and the importance of caring for it. However, as childhood memories resurfaced into my conscious mind, I found myself basking in great delight and awe.

## Story of Grandpa Wong

Memories of Wong Gung Gung (Grandpa Wong) popped into my mind recently. He was not my blood grandfather, but our connection was deep. I was a lucky child to have the love and attention of the merry band of best pals that my maternal grandfather always had surrounding him. Grandpa Wong was one of them. Although he was significantly more quiet and timid than the other elderly gentlemen, Grandpa Wong and I shared a peaceful, private understanding between us, even with our differences in temperament. I was the outgoing, hyperactive little person, and my insatiable curiosity often took me places where others had no interest.

One afternoon while everyone else was busy talking and eating, Grandpa Wong remained alone in his bedroom, and I snuck away from the group to be with him. Sitting very still in a lotus position with his legs crossed and eyes closed, he neither spoke nor moved. I barely breathed while my eyes remained glued on him. Wait—he must have moved. There seemed to be a small space between his body and the bed. Floating just slightly above the mattress, he became perfectly still in midair.

This must have continued for quite some time. At one point, my mother came into the room. As she pulled me out and closed the door behind us, my mother whispered, "Wong Gung Gung is meditating. You mustn't disturb him." She then explained that he needed his time alone to concentrate on his exercises, so that he could continue doing amazing things. His level of discipline and cultivation was that of a Kung Fu master, able to leap high into the air like a giant bird. "Wong Gung Gung can jump from a wall over ten feet high and practically fly," she told me. He was like those men and women in Kung Fu movies, leaping to high places and back down. Cool, huh?

Although I do not have specific memories of Grandpa Wong teaching me how to meditate and gather the Chi within me, my young body picked up his signals and recorded his vibrations. A kind and gentle man, he carried himself with modesty and humility. I believe that he prayed for me and protected me in his own quiet way. Even though he died more than three decades ago, I still find many images of him flashing through my mind at very opportune moments. Sensing his presence and recalling memories of him fills me with great honor. I feel extremely blessed to have had him in my life when he was alive—and now. ☙

## Story of Whispering Trees

Fast-forward to sometime in the late 1990s and you will find me racing against the fast-moving storm clouds threatening to dump snow onto the entire Lake Tahoe region, a beautiful mountainous area of Northern California. Picture me driving a light-blue Toyota pickup truck taking the zigzagging curves through the mountains on Highway 50. Around one of the curves, I suddenly blow a tire, but there is no shoulder of the road to pull over and change the flat for almost a quarter of a mile.

This experience was harrowing and got my adrenaline pumping, to say the least. By some miracle I was able to find a spot and pull over safely. Racing against the storm, I jumped out of the truck and pulled out my tire-changing tools and spare tire. One by one I took off the lug nuts—all but the very last. This one would not budge. I put both feet on the tire iron and bounced up and down with all my weight on it, but it would not loosen one bit. Then I put on my ski boots and stepped on that tire iron with full confidence that I could crank the last nut loose under the weight of my entire body. No success. I looked around. Cars and trucks zoomed by me without stopping. Everyone was racing to escape the threatening dark snow clouds. No one slowed down to help; I was truly invisible to them.

Still facing the road, I suddenly heard whispering voices behind me. I whipped around to see where they came from, but there was nobody. I was surrounded by nothing but pine trees. Out of the side of my eye, I saw the tops of the trees to my right sway back and forth in synchronicity. They whispered to me, "You know what to do." Huh? What? My goodness—I was hearing trees talking and was definitely nuts.

What I wanted was to get that last lug nut off, throw on my tire, and get out of there. But I heard it again, "You know what to do." Overwhelmed and frustrated, I had no clue what to do. All of a sudden, I spread my feet apart, bent my knees, and got into a Horse Stance—a body position in martial arts which I had never had the patience to learn like my cousins had. I then took a deep breath in through my nose and lifted my arms out and up, reaching for the sky. Slowly, I exhaled while bringing my hands down and passing them in front of my face, chest, stomach, and down to just below my belly button.

As fast as I fell into this trance, I snapped out of it, jumped up, and stepped on the tire iron again. On the first bounce the nut instantly came loose. I could not believe it but quickly and gratefully changed the tire. Standing back up to get into the truck, I turned around and faced the trees that had guided me. With a respectful bow of the head, my lips whispered a quiet "thank you" to them. That was how I beat the storm. ∽

## Magical Power of Gut Intuition

I truly believe that we all have a magical strength within us. Most athletes, firefighters, neurosurgeons, and people who care for newborn babies automatically access this power every single day. They trust their instincts to guide them, listening to knowledge that comes from beyond their conscious minds. I love observing how their mind-body-spirit connection puts them into a trance-like state and enables them to perform incredible feats. It is as if angels are lifting their bodies upward and telepathically sending them the exact information they need to know and what to do. How awesome!

When I watch a snowboarder jump, twist, and flip in the air I can feel my abdominal muscles contract with the tuck and release upon landing. Rock climbers also have this trust and connection with the energy in their bodies and the boulders they climb. They hold deep respect for gravity, breath, and movement at the microscopic level and even the cellular level. When we move and regulate the flow of Chi within us, we can maximize the potential of our human bodies at any moment, anytime and anywhere. Willingness to explore what we have within us is key, and courage to bring forth our gifts is golden.

Accessing and fine-tuning our natural gut intuition—present even before birth—is vital to making great decisions for our well-being. By developing trust in our intuition, we grow to appreciate its value to guide us in every direction we take. Following our gut feeling is living harmoniously within ourselves. When I used to listen to my head and ignore my gut, I ended up in countless undesirable places. Now quieting my overworked mind minimizes mental clutter, protects me from electro-magnetic interference, and allows my body to return to homeostasis—its natural state of balance. *AH!* That feels yummy. ∞

Our gut feelings can bring us into alignment with our true selves and lead us to wondrous results the conscious mind could never dream up. When deliberately staying focused and on track, we unblock constipation and allow Chi to flow freely, which dissipates temptation to pursue any immediate gratification that distracts us from enjoying our gifts and talents and enables us to live on purpose.

I am boldly stating that we are born with an incredible power within us that is at our disposal. What do we *do* with what we have? In desperate physical pain and emotional distress I have learned to acknowledge, respect, and access my natural ability to improve the flow of Chi within me. Reversing the feelings of restlessness, a foreboding sense of uncertainty about surroundings, and vulnerability to emotional and physical pain, I have become robust in many ways. By striving to keep my internal organs and systems happy, I enjoy freedom from most everything that used to irritate me. My connection and collaboration with the Universe is a lot of fun. I have become a duck that barely notices any water rolling down its back. From where I sit, waddling sounds pretty good to me. ∞

## Dialing into My Dan Tian

Allow me to back up for one second. Prior to seven-and-a-half years ago, we would not have been having this conversation, for I refused to engage in woo-woo subjects like this. Yes, you could have offered me physical therapy, personal training, and prescription medication. But my face would have gone blank at the mention of energy cysts, chakras, chi gong, craniosacral therapy, muscle testing, goji berries, kale, meridians, tapping—and more.

It was not that I had never heard these words before, but my mind compartmentalized much of what I learned from my ancestors during my younger years and shut the door on those memories until several years ago. I deliberately chose traditional Western Medicine over Eastern wisdom and practices. Then something shifted. Memories of intrinsic knowledge of ancient concepts, disciplines, and truths from early childhood re-energized me. A series of events and "a-ha" moments woke me up from a deep slumber I had been in for most of my adulthood. Deeply grateful for the bubbling up of countless images and impressions, I found these experiences to be delightful, sweet, and rich.

One of my subconscious recollections was that of Chi Gong. What continuously amazes me about this Chinese art of moving energy throughout our bodies is its simplicity and power. We can use our very own body parts and breath to improve the flow of energy throughout our systems and regain balance, stability, immune health, and even youth. Personally, the combination of Chi Gong and meridian tapping has offered me greater balance and stability than I had even dared to imagine. As I grew healthier, my body released nearly thirty pounds. My body, not my mind, taught me how to eliminate what did not belong—without surgery, diets, or programs. Looking younger every year was not in my plan either, but I can live with that.

Embracing memories of my ancestors floating into my consciousness, I honor my Dan Tian, a special space just below my belly button and inward. It is my center, the home of my soul, where my body is connected to everything that is bigger and beyond what I am. Each one of us has a Dan Tian, where our gut intuition resides, right about where our intestines and diaphragm muscle for deep breathing and powerful singing are. **Picture your spiritual umbilical cord to the Universe, connecting your Dan Tian to the sky, stars, and galaxies beyond. Imagine receiving light, energy, strength, information, and wisdom into it, allowing you to expand and flourish on Earth.**

My belief is that each time I take a deep breath from this area, I am linking my earthling body to an energy source in the celestial realm that is generous, wise, and protective. It is no mistake or coincidence that our spiritual connection with the Universe is merely inches away from where our umbilical cords once supplied vital nutrients to us while we were in our mothers' wombs.

For the record, I have not always been this emotionally sober or spiritual about taking care of my stomach area, especially the lower abdomen.

Since my youth, I resented my tummy for being too big and keeping me from buttoning my pants. A little girl in ballet class, I was a huge target for repeated reminders to suck in my gut. It took so much effort to look good and move gracefully with this belly of mine. Even when yo-yo diets helped to reveal somewhat of a waistline, my lower belly continued to stick out. Because of the way I ate, I earned my nicknames, "Whale Blubber" and "Tub of Lard." ∞

My early days were tough, but my journey only got harder as I entered puberty and early adulthood. Ugly memories of bullying, abuse, and exclusion would still be affecting me deeply if it were not for my intense work through Chi Gong and meridian tapping. Dismantling the unsettling power of shame, embarrassment, guilt, and self-loathing at the cellular level did wonders for me in building self-respect and self-confidence. Today, the negative charge is gone, replaced by my willingness to adopt healthy habits. My tendency to do what is beneficial for me has skyrocketed. After overcoming our subconscious resistance to change, we can reap unlimited benefits from positive affirmations and action plans. Releasing trauma and emotional baggage must happen at the cellular level for happy, long-term recovery and vitality for the rest of our lives.

With a variety of energy-based tools, I have made peace with my tummy, and it loves me back, too. By reconciling with this very important area of my body, I have a strong relationship with my stomach, liver, and other digestive organs and am far more present to address their needs throughout the day. **Taking good care of my intestines, I now enjoy astounding mental clarity, a far more robust immune system, and sharpened gut intuition that gives me a direct connect to the Universe.** Because of all this, I am able to use time more wisely, pace my exertion of energy, and enjoy the many kinds of prosperity my heart is willing to receive. I shine brightly with faith and confidence—even when I am in pain—and rely upon my gut intuition to nurture all my relationships with family, friends, healthcare professionals, business people, and community leaders. ☭

Today, my healthy choices bring good vibrations to everyone around me. I have fun and laugh a lot, whether I am by myself or with others. This also is a gift from something that is beyond yet within me. My resilient body is filled with wisdom to heal and execute amazing processes, like circulating blood and delivering nutrients, allowing me to breathe easily and protecting me from pathogens that do not belong in me. While asleep or awake, my systems do a great job of digesting and absorbing nutrients and eliminating waste to give birth to vibrant new cells.

My body certainly deserves a standing ovation! How about yours? Let us send good vibrations to one another and ask our bodies what we need to do to reach the next level of performance in conscious and subconscious activities each and every day.

Reflect upon the beauty, youth, and energy you were born with and invite them into the present. Amazing things will happen! ∞

## Exercise for Chapter Five

*Ilana's Mindfulness Meditation and Tapping Exercise for HONORING INTERNAL ORGANS in a 5-Part Format (adapted Progressive Energy Field Tapping or Pro EFT\*)*

Below are passages you may reflect on as you breathe deeply (**CG**) in silent meditation or say the words aloud while relaxing and tapping together the SIDES of both palms of your hands—the "karate chop point" (KC Point). *(See APPENDIX A: Tapping Meridian Points.)*

Please remember to drink some water before, during, and after this exercise.

❖    Reversal 1: "Even though my missing a strong connection with my internal organs is keeping me from feeling fantastic in my body, there is a part of me that doesn't want to face this for whatever reason. I'm not ready to sit still, listen, and trust, but I want to love and accept myself anyway." **CG**

❖    Reversal 2: "Even though my thinking too much and being confused about which paths to take prevents me from sleeping and functioning well, there is a part of me that still wants to hold on to the chaos, rely on the brain between my ears, and ignore my gut intuition. But I want to love, accept, and honor myself anyway." **CG**

❖ Reversal 3: "Even though my ignoring the significance of my pain and telling my body how it should behave still blocks me from getting real relief, there is a part of me that is ready to give my internal organs my loyalty and appropriate care. And I want that part to win! Because I love and accept myself." ○ㅅ

❖ Reversal 4: "Even though my remaining doubts about what my body is saying prevent me from taking action to feel fantastic in my body, I choose to breathe deeply often, talk to my amazing internal organs each day, and listen to what my gut intuition tells me. I love and accept myself deeply and completely." ○ㅅ

❖ CHOICE Statement: "I choose to enjoy a loving relationship with my internal organs and allow my intuition to guide me, so that I can feel fantastic in my body, honor my presence on this planet, and share my laughter and vibrancy with others. And I deeply and completely love and accept myself." ○ㅅ

*\*Pro EFT™ (Progressive Energy Field Tapping™) and the process of reversal neutralization or "Reversal Setup" were developed by EFT Master Lindsay Kenny.*

# CHAPTER SIX

# My Bridge to Vibrancy

## Embracing the Pain

I am in love with a piece of good news for your body and mine: our bodies *want* to and *can* heal when we give them the space, love, and time to do so. "Yes, maybe for you but not for me," was my immediate reaction when I heard this while lying on the massage table of my craniosacral therapist's office. With sadness and anger, I heard my brain pout, "This pain feels like it's *never* going away—can't even *think* about being healed. I just want the pain to STOP!"

With less than four years in 12-step recovery at that time, I had already lost several dear friends to alcohol, cancer, and suicide. As dastardly as the emotional pain was, nothing had broken me yet, until CRPS mercilessly almost blew me out of the water. But the big Universe stepped in and put me on that craniosacral table to discover deeper levels of self-compassion. Even to this day, it still perplexes me as to how I ended up on that table—as I did not even know what craniosacral therapy was. "Cranio" pertains to the skull, and "sacral" refers to the tailbone area at the base of our spine. Beyond that I drew a blank. How did I find this therapist? Probably from a healing arts directory, but I do not recall ever having one or dialing a number for an appointment. In hindsight I did and said many things I have no recollection of; intense brain fog— even without the presence of prescription narcotics, alcohol, or street drugs—came with the severe pain.

Perhaps I should also tell you that abstract, touchy-feely stuff was not my cup of tea. Massaging muscles for relief I understood, but moving the bones behind my eye sockets (sphenoid) and releasing adhesions and soft-tissue around my tailbone (sacrum) seemed very weird to me. That which had *not* been in my field of vision prior to being on this table suddenly became my whole world. Now very important to me was caring for all the bone, cartilage, and other matter, including the sac of fluid (cerebrospinal fluid) protecting my brain and critical parts of the nervous system in my spine.

Whatever the Universe was thinking when it got me onto this table, I am truly grateful for this gift that came to me in spite of myself. This was not solely about medical intervention; I needed an up-close and personal education about my connection to the vast Universe—and this was where I began to receive it. Releasing dastardly pain required that I commit to honoring cell life within this body, occupying space in my vessel with a real sense of ownership, and being on this planet to embrace limitless possibilities. To feel stronger and healthier,

I learned to stop living in my head. Relying upon human intellect was *not* the ticket to freedom. *GULP.* My efforts to ignore pain—in hopes that it would disappear on its own—wasted much of my energy and time. Willpower alone could not decrease the intensity of pain for more than two-and-a-half seconds. Keeping busy with other activities, to avoid feeling useless, worked for only short periods of time. My body needed the *real* me—the person I was born to be—savoring each present moment. This was the wisdom to which I awakened.

There I was on that table. "Embrace the pain in your body," my craniosacral therapist said to me. Huh? What? Come again? Why would I want to embrace something that was driving me crazy? That idea *alone* was insane. Eventually, I began to understand what she was asking of me. A child calls for help when he or she needs our attention, comfort, or love. Children, much like us, want to feel safe, secure, and remembered. They are willing to protect those they love, like their pets, favorite toys, and friends. When sensing something not quite right, they alert us in their own special way, so that everyone they cherish can remain together in safety. ✇

The same holds true for physical pain. My body was calling for attention to issues with my bones, muscles, soft tissues, and nerves. However, my mind went to places where it did not belong, such as fantasizing about diving frantically into rehabilitation therapy with hopes of getting right back to work. *My* plans for the present or future did not include breath-sucking pain, crutches, wheelchairs, walkers, and canes. Up to this point, I had meditated every morning for spiritual growth and addiction recovery, but using meditation for listening to what my body parts were saying? I was not ready for that. Yet, it became my full-time job from which amazing results emerged.

I soon realized that paying attention to pain in my body was like listening closely to a struggling child in need of attention. Thus, making amends to every part of my body was truly worthwhile in time and effort. "Body-Part Reconciliation™" (BPR) became a wonderful strategy I developed and used to harvest peace in my body's inner garden. Using some of the basic principles in Chinese medicine and meridian tapping, I began to feed energy into where my body needed support.

For example, during periods of extreme stress, the energy of fear is trapped in our kidneys. By tapping or sending vibration into the area just below the pointy parts of the collarbones, below our throats (CB Point), we stimulate points along the kidney meridian. Adapting the beautiful ancient Hawaiian prayer *Ho'oponopono,* I tap and say, "Thank you, kidneys, for cleaning my blood. I'm sorry you've had to work so hard. Please forgive me for allowing fear and stress to affect you. I love you, kidneys—the left one and the right one!" ∾

Layer by layer, my tapping conversations released the scrambled, reversed, and stuck energy caused by physical and emotional injuries my body had been carrying into the present moment. Every cell in the buds, leaves, stems, trunks, and roots in my body garden began to respond to my voice, touch, and mental images. As I continued making direct and living amends to the weaker parts of my body, they healed faster and got stronger.

I discovered that my body had so very much to say to me. Having suffered intense trauma, it needed the brain between my ears to calm down. "Shhh! Stay quiet not only *on* the table, but everywhere *else!*" my body begged me. As you can imagine, this was an extremely tall order for my already bruised-ego-of-a-brain. I swallowed hard and took a back seat to allow my body and its own brain to do the rebuilding. My entire body garden needed space to rest and relax. Learning the art of relaxation required practice, but as it became a part of my daily self-care regimen of healthy habits, I got happier. This on-going growth process still continues to lift me into higher levels of comfort and serenity. And look at me now!

I chose to practice remaining quiet enough to listen for my body's needs because of the many *unappealing* alternatives presented to me. What probably lit my butt to explore touchy-feely, whatchamacallit healing stuff were numerous discussions with my doctors about their implanting a spinal cord stimulator (SCS) into my spine to manage nerve-pain sensitivity. I had always thought of myself as pretty high up on the macho bravery scale.

But I nearly vomited at the thought of "the box." As if *on cue*, the Universe brought three people into my life that had had these spinal surgeries and periodically went under the knife to have new batteries installed in their implants. I found this solution neither sexy nor enticing. Maybe the brochures needed work. ○₰

Discussions about other devices, injections, pills, and so on made amputation sound good—but with that, phantom pain would still remain after removing my foot. Soldiers with CRPS and amputated legs and arms know what I mean. For me, taking narcotic prescription medication was a no go. I even signed a form that would not permit anyone to dispense narcotics to me. When given the opportunity to reunite with my old friends Mary and Jane (marijuana), I waved my hand and shook my head "ONT!"—Oh, No Thanks! Even though pot was available in pill form, I did not want to give myself an excuse to spend even one minute escaping from my life or fantasizing about the good old days. This, too, was not a solution; my life was complicated enough.

In short, my gift of desperation came in an elaborately wrapped package. Debilitating, identity-shattering, and ego-bruising pain led me to become very present with my bones, muscles, cartilage, and all types of body tissue I could not see or feel. Freedom from this misery required that I acknowledge, embrace, and respect the pain *before* it could decrease in intensity, duration, and frequency in the long run.

I will say it again: this was a full-time job. A tremendous amount of hard work it was, stretching me far beyond my comfort zone, but the outcomes have been worth it. I was serious about my personal pledge to go to any lengths to protect my physical and emotional sobriety. And the Universe responded with gifts that were beyond what I had ever dared to imagine. I am here; so are you. What a gift! ❧

## Plenty of Options

Twelve-step recovery taught and showed me that I always have more options than I think. Holding on to this belief, I persevered in exploring choices previously not visible to me. For this wisdom and its practical application I am eternally grateful. The combination of physical and emotional sobriety has taken me to many wonderful places, and I look forward to witnessing many more miracles.

My world is so expansive, with doors wide open to fields and modalities I barely knew existed before, including Functional Medicine, Kinesiology and Applied Kinesiology, Naturopathic Medicine and Homeopathy, Meridian Energy Techniques, Somatic Therapy, Neuromuscular Massage Therapy, Energy Psychology and Medicine, Ayurveda, and others.

Searching far and wide for options that would work for me invited beautiful, loving souls who gave me hope for my life when I barely had any. Struggling with multiple health issues and the medical bills that came with them, I watched my savings dwindle to nothing. Unable to work,

I did a lot of soul-searching and developed a new perspective on money that helped me make good financial decisions while rehabilitating my body. As money is *energy*, investing it into my body for greater health opens more opportunities for receiving and giving. ✂

Good habits of recording my spending and picking up the phone to explore payment options that worked for me were invaluable. Daily "visions" meditations on desirable outcomes, while I was immobile, helped me regain my ability to travel, dance, and enjoy many other pleasurable activities. I believed wholeheartedly that my dreams—however small or grand—could come to fruition, one bite-sized action at a time. My mentors in 12-step recovery guided me through some very tough periods, and I am glad I followed their strange suggestions, trusted the Universe, and broke through many comfort zones, one by one.

Despite the physical pain that was intense enough that I became willing to surrender my foot, I found hope for a better present that offered me an even more promising future. Through all my brain-fog issues and loss of memory, I knew I was put on Earth not only to survive but to thrive, just like you. Whether you are reading or listening to this book right now, you were put on this planet to be here *at this very moment* in time. It may sound too simplistic, but the truth is simple. Thank you for being here—I mean it. ✂

# Ilana's One Thing

People often ask me, "What is the *one thing* I could do to rebuild my body like yours?" I *could* suggest that you drink two to three cups of warm-to-hot water first thing every morning, which is terrific for flushing out waste in our internal organs, giving them a great energetic boost to function more efficiently throughout the day. If we feel great taking a shower after waking up, why not give our insides a nice warm/hot shower too? Our bodies certainly deserve this!

Or I *could* encourage you to take three deep breaths—inhale through your nose and exhale through your lips—when you wake up, before every meal, and at bedtime. Engaging the diaphragm muscle in your lower abdomen gives your internal organs a great massage, increases oxygen supply to the brain and body, and effectively eliminates carbon dioxide waste. This stress and anxiety-reduction exercise offers us better hormonal balance, fewer mood swings, and higher productivity throughout the day. Great goals to have! Go ahead—take three deep breaths now. I'll wait. ೞ ೞ ೞ

I do have many other quick-but-powerful suggestions throughout this book, but keep this one thing in mind: **From the time you wake up until you go to bed, <u>listen</u> to the genius brain of your body and <u>encourage</u> its healthy flow of blood, breath, nutrients, waste, and energy. In short— happy organs, happy life!**

Listen to the genius brain of your body. When we give our body a voice and follow its guidance, our internal battles begin to dissipate. Our nervous systems do not enjoy carrying memories of shame, guilt, or regret and need our cooperation in letting them go. More specifically, whenever I see people holding "Stand Up to Cancer" signs or "Stand Up for (name of their loved one)," I want to shout, "Let's stand up to self-battery!" At the cellular level our bodies store memories of our negative self-talk, self-deprecation, and self-deprivation of nutrients, rest, and sunshine. They also remember the times we ignore our needs and put others' needs ahead of our own. Let us turn this around to strengthen our immune systems. Lovingly shake loose and melt away all the agitation, anger, resentment, shame, guilt, and regret. Aim for emotional sobriety and self-compassion! ❃

Encourage a healthy flow of blood, breath, nutrients, waste, and energy throughout your body. Have confidence that each cell of your body knows what it does and does not need. Learn to listen, gauge, and take action in response to what is happening. Our needs do continuously change, whether or not we are ready for them. For me, some medications worked well for a while, but as my body and mental attitude changed, my doctors adjusted the dosages or switched to others. Complex health issues require that we remain open to modifying the combination of solutions to create new ones. Staying flexible (mentally and emotionally) helped me regain greater range of motion in most of my joints. How amazing! And energetically, the combination of physical flexibility and open-mindedness opened doors to even more possibilities. Two words: Yummy freedom!

There was not one pill, one person, one procedure, or one technique that magically improved my health. However, I was steadfast in overcoming any resistance to adopting new solutions and habits. Change can be challenging and unsettling, but grab onto the good stuff. Remember that you always have more options than you think. Just *F.L.O.W.—Feel Light Offering Wisdom.* ⌨

## 7 Key Ingredients for Vibrancy

To me, vibrancy is the glow of the dancing flame in our soul that shines within us so brightly that people can see it on the outside. Feeling vibrant, inside and out, requires collaborative teamwork among our minds, hearts, gut instincts, bodies, and souls—all connected to the vast Universe. This is deliberate recovery. Remember that a football team needs more than just the quarterback, and a baseball team requires more than a pitcher. Every team must have a coach, and any game without a referee or umpire spells disaster. When we stretch our bodies and reach beyond our physical selves, every part of us can function with greater ease, strength, and confidence.

When our internal organs are flowing and happily doing their jobs, we are better equipped to handle stress and perform activities at higher levels.

Staying robust is crucial, as any physiological or internal struggle can disrupt our nervous systems and produce a domino effect that makes living less enjoyable. If one or more of our internal organs feels uncomfortable, malnourished, or threatened, our brain can lose its ability to process information efficiently and accurately. We need be cautious about not overtaxing our body and brain, because stress keeps us from making clear, effective decisions.

Choosing our thoughts, words, and actions with mindfulness will minimize the frequency and intensity of perceived negative experiences that can flood our systems with sadness, grief, and anger. All this heavy energy slows down our productivity at the cellular level. Physically, our immune systems get weaker; emotionally, we lose hormonal balance; and mentally, declining gastrointestinal health leads to longer and more frequent periods of brain fog and unnatural memory loss. *BLAH!*

The depth of my misery challenged me to answer these questions: "Are you willing to go to any lengths to keep your internal organs happy? What will you do to feel safe and at peace and to laugh with real joy on this planet—no matter what is happening around you?" I had to look inward and ask, "What am I willing to do to make peace with my entire body, not just parts of it, so that I can travel the world, lift spirits high, and flourish like I was meant to in the first place?"

There was not one book, movie, or course that taught me how to overcome the many limitations of my illness. However, these *7 Key Ingredients for Vibrancy* helped me turn my life around when I finally committed to attaining higher levels of passion, fervor, and joy on Earth. Adopting these practices and principles, I rose to vibrancy one day at a time.

**7 Key Ingredients for Vibrancy**

1. I face brutal truths about my health conditions and take personal responsibility for voicing my needs.

2. I embrace a growth mindset that moves me from groaning to glowing and allow the Universe to guide me through an abundance of options.

3. I rise above obstacles that limit my physical space within and around my body by eliminating toxins and foods that my body does not need and releasing mental and emotional triggers at a cellular level.

4. I accept love and support from an entire village of healthcare and healing professionals, family, friends, and neighbors.

5. I develop self-compassion for individual body parts, internal organs, and my entire being by creating time to heal and celebrate each bit of progress.

6. I live life on purpose and wholeheartedly embrace that there is plenty.

7. I continuously commit to being a walking, talking Self-Care Vigilante who serves others with integrity and balance. ℭℨ

Throughout my personal journey, these *7 Key Ingredients for Vibrancy* rose above other strategies for restoration and recovery. In fact, while writing and editing this book, I am using all seven of these key ingredients to support my physical, mental, emotional, and spiritual alignment with self and the Universe. Collaborative teamwork within and all around me is bringing this book to life—what a blessing! Creative projects can take us to new levels of awareness and greater sense of purpose, especially when we stay connected to and support our bodies. Let us pay attention to *every* part of us while we contribute to the greater good of all! ℭℨ

# Exercise for Chapter Six

*Ilana's Mindfulness Meditation and Tapping Exercise for EMBRACING INTUITION in a 5 -Part Format (adapted Progressive Energy Field Tapping or Pro EFT\*)*

Below are passages you may reflect on as you breathe deeply (**ꙮ**) in silent meditation or say the words aloud while relaxing and tapping together the SIDES of both palms of your hands—the "karate chop point" (KC Point). *(See APPENDIX A: Tapping Meridian Points.)*

Please remember to drink some water before, during, and after this exercise.

❖ Reversal 1: "Even though searching for solutions and making tough decisions every day keep me from fully relaxing and enjoying life, there is a part of me that doesn't want to let go of the drama or agony—for whatever reason, conscious or subconscious. (Maybe I'm comfortable in confusion, afraid of making mistakes, or can't trust my decisions or anyone else's.) But I want to love and accept myself anyway." **ꙮ**

❖ Reversal 2: "Even though my uncertainty, confusion, or overwhelm about which health expert and what information to trust blocks me from making great progress, there is a part of me that wants to rely solely on my brain and ignore my gut intuition. (Maybe I believe I have to try *everything*, or I'm afraid *of* getting better or not getting better.) But I want to love, accept, and honor myself anyway." ❧

❖ Reversal 3: "Even though a part of me still tries to control my body and tell it what to do without listening to my gut intuition, there is another part of me that is willing to slow down and hear what my body needs to tell me. I want that part to win, because I love and accept myself." ❧

❖ Reversal 4: "Even though this remaining doubt about whether to trust myself or others holds me back from *living in* the best solutions, I choose to breathe deeply, dial into my Dan Tian, and embrace my gut intuition—downloaded wisdom from the Universe—one day at a time. I love and accept myself deeply and completely." ❧

❖ CHOICE Statement: "I choose to listen carefully to my internal organs and allow my mind and gut intuition to work collaboratively in accessing divine guidance. My vision is to grow stronger in my body, always celebrate my presence on this planet, and serve others with my vibrant inner light and power. I do love and accept myself deeply and completely." ❧

*Pro EFT™ (Progressive Energy Field Tapping™) and the process of reversal neutralization or "Reversal Setup" were developed by EFT Master Lindsay Kenny.*

# CHAPTER SEVEN:

# First Three Ingredients

As you already know, I think a lot about food—including thinking about food often and thinking highly of it. Thank goodness I no longer eat all the food I think about or think about food I have not yet had the pleasure of meeting.

Have no worries. As obsessive as the aforementioned paragraph may sound, in the remaining chapters I take you further along in my journey that expands much broader than my former love affair with that f-word. In addition to stories, I present key ingredients that brought me to where I am now. This is not a textbook, reference guide, or manual, but I am happy to share with you what worked for me—even during times when I thought I was sliding backward but was actually gaining progress. Please take what you like and leave the rest, but keep in mind that whenever you are ready to explore this in greater depth, you can pick up this book again or listen to the upcoming audiobook. See what works best for you. Are you ready? Good. Let's go! ☎

1. I face brutal truths about my health conditions and take personal responsibility for voicing my needs.

2. I create a growth mindset that moves me from groaning to glowing and allow the Universe to guide me through an abundance of options.

3. I rise above obstacles that limit my physical space within and around my body by eliminating toxins and irritating foods and releasing mental and emotional triggers at a cellular level. ℭ

# Ingredient 1:

## HONESTY AND RESPONSIBILITY
*Facing Brutal Truth and Taking Personal Responsibility*

I had to face the brutal truth about my health and take personal responsibility for voicing my needs. Pretending that my health issues were not so serious was as productive as towel drying a car in the rain. Being in denial and embarrassed about how awful I felt and looked did not serve me well. With each new diagnosis my immediate reaction was "How could I possibly have this condition? You must be wrong!" Denial was a natural, human response that helped me cope with bad news. When the light bulb in my head came on, my next thought was "Gee, no wonder I've been feeling like crap!"

Next, anger within me began to boil until I raged: "How did I get this? Who did this to me?" Wanting to point my finger and blame someone—even God—was my knee-jerk reaction. After the rage subsided, sadness set in. Wallowed in feelings of shame, guilt, remorse, and self-pity, I isolated myself and played my cards close to my chest. Doing this was exactly *opposite* of what was critical to my rehabilitation and sense of worthiness on this planet. ❧

For almost four-and-a-half decades of my life, the conversation sounded like this: whenever someone asked if they could pick up something for me at the store, I automatically replied, "I need a new body." They always laughed, but I was serious. "The body you have now is the only one you're ever going to get" was the stark truth they put before me. That news was so depressing because I wanted out of this one. Repairing broken parts and pieces became excruciating, exhausting, and frustrating. I faced unpredictable flare-ups, and every single one of my conditions tested my spiritual fitness—CRPS, migraine headaches, chronic sinus infections, tinnitus "silent reflux" with esophageal erosion and vocal cord dysphonia, fibromyalgia, asthma, allergies, hypermobility syndrome, shingles, depression, and other subtle and not-so-subtle maladies. Many of them challenged my decision to refuse narcotic painkillers or anything else that might jeopardize the physical and emotional sobriety I so enjoyed.

With the complication of multiple physical and mental health issues, I was holding on to hope by an extremely thin thread during the first four years of having CRPS. Did my pain create hopelessness, or did hopelessness cause pain? Whichever came first did not matter. The egg and chicken both arrived. My point is that pain and hopelessness were intertwined like roots in a quagmire, and to get out of it required my active participation and complete commitment to living in this body—no matter what. The old "fake it until you make it" strategy could not hide CRPS; seeing myself as a victim gained sympathy from others but deepened the pain. Camping on my pity pot bred bitterness while I watched other people smile through life. My staying small and nearly invisible was spiritually criminal, like saying "No thanks" to all the love, talents, and gifts the Universe had offered me. ⌘

As I changed one thing—everything—rebuilding my body was not a physical job but a spiritual one. For whatever reasons that led to my not wanting this body and asking for a new one from the store, I had to stop seeing myself as broken (needing repair) and begin embracing that I—despite the many detours and distractions—was created to be a wonderful source of light, healing, and laughter. The intensity of chronic pain and its not-so-nice surprise flare-ups continue to call attention to my body, but I see them as necessary temporary challenges that ignite positive action toward spiritual growth. **Although breathing deeply into the pain can be extremely exhausting, and the search for comfortable body positions may seem near-**

ly impossible at times, my vision is to create a long-lasting series of fantastic new moments, each better than the one before.

Looking back, I now see that my health could have gotten progressively worse if I had not been brutally honest with myself and others and taken personal responsibility for making significant changes to overcome the dastardly combination of pain, mental fatigue, and depression. With every ounce of honesty and integrity I could muster, I pursued physical rehabilitation with my focus on spiritual fitness and growth. Yours truly took off the mask of bravado and machismo and dropped the "Don't worry about me, I'm fine" attitude to replace it with the willingness to nurture and nourish every part of me.

I set aside my "know-it-all-ism" and asked my brain to step back and allow my body to speak freely about what it truly needed. My inner light emerged as I began to release raw feelings of shame, guilt, remorse, embarrassment, and unworthiness that had been buried deep in the cells and pathways of my nervous systems. Not easy was dismantling the distorted pair of glasses through which I saw myself and viewed the world, but it had to happen. Good news—it worked! ◌

# Ingredient 2:

## MINDSET AND GUIDANCE
*Embrace a Growth Mindset and Allow the Universe to Guide*

From groaning to glowing, I regained my ability to speak and write from a place of vibrancy and serenity, which was nothing short of a miracle. I had to dump my false self-perception of being a broken person and adopt a healing-and-growth mindset. Embracing my abundance of wonderful options to choose from was critical in leaving behind my minimalistic existence of continuous pain and anguish. These days, although I still experience bad pain days and numerous physical limitations, my body reassures me that it is releasing, readjusting, and shifting so that we may move into the next stage of healing and growth. I trust it and listen to its wisdom.

In case you were wondering, I did hit a rock bottom, a desperate moment that made a huge difference in my recovery. A person who was always assisting others, I became someone who needed a tremendous amount of help. Here it is: being the patient was the hardest pill for me to swallow. Needing people around to care for me, clean my home, do my shopping, and help me think logically nearly killed me. Although I had a tankful of gasoline in my car, I was not able drive it for over a year. Believing that I had little to offer anyone because I was sick, boring, and burdensome, I stopped dating and making new friends for a long while. ☙

Thankfully, the pain in my body ignited a remarkable revolution and forced me to make a decision: I could either drown in the quagmire of tangled hopelessness and pain or choose to be a phoenix that rises up from the ashes and soars across the sky. The latter vision sent a powerful surge of healing energy throughout my body, and I woke up: "Here I am!" Leaving behind my "broke mindset" (I am broken—hear me roar!), I began to stretch beyond my comfort zone with a completely different mindset and embark on a new path filled with passion and respect for life.

"How does she stay on this great path?" you may be wondering. On days that I have difficulty walking or sitting, I deliberately banish self-pity, judgment, and anger. Instead of scolding my body for failing me, I now thank it for offering me more one-on-one time with the Universe. **This is my most prized possession: my intimate connection with my Creator and access to deeper bonding moments with the Universe at any time. I have a priceless sanctuary that is mine forever—a spiritual place of nourishment for my enjoyment, no matter where I am physically, mentally, or emotionally.** Even when pain is very uncomfortable, I know that beauty will always emerge as long as I keep my eyes and heart open. Remaining optimistic and resilient during difficult times, I continuously choose to celebrate as many heartwarming moments as possible. My hope is that you will, too.

If you are not optimistic yet, know that my adopting a mindset that lifted me to new heights was not a quick overnight process. I was stunned, dazed, and humiliated as CRPS knocked me out in the very first round of our boxing match. With tremendous pain and brain fog I somehow found an organization called Reflex Sympathetic Dystrophy Syndrome Association (RSDSA, www.rsds.org), picked up the phone, and spoke to the kind voice of a generous gentleman who allowed me to stumble over my words as I told him about my diagnosis. He sent me information in print that confirmed I was not alone or imagining this nightmare.

So in spite of myself, I began to accept the Universe's gift of love from people who understood, like a pain support group. You can as well. Reading this book is a great first step. Then, pick up the phone to talk to people who are in a support group or who face similar issues. I still do not recall how I found my local chapter of the American Chronic Pain Association (ACPA, www.theacpa.org), but the flow of gratitude within me runs deep. My new friends taught me how to be a patient advocate for myself, to speak up when I was hurting, and to ask for what I needed. They coached me on how to ask questions and be persistent in exploring medical treatment options. When I was tired and wanted to give up, they kept cheering me on and loving me, and they still do, to this day. ೞ

By honoring the principles and tools of 12-step recovery in the face of brutal pain and injured body parts, I gained a feeling of greater spiritual connectedness both within me and beyond my physical self. *Living* the steps, principles, and tools, I began making amends to each internal organ and body part which manifested countless blessings. No longer did I think or say that my injured parts were "bad," "weak," or "defective." Instead, I reclaimed them with statements like "My feet and hips are calling for my love and attention" or "My arms and hands deserve some TLC!" Body-part reconciliation not only stirred creative energy within and around me but also improved my relationships with people in all areas of my life. Interesting phenomenon: when I take better care of *me*, you benefit. Good deal.

Through the grace and mercy of the Universe, my new mindset replaced resentments and resistance with compassion and confidence. What an incredible way to live on this planet! By taking personal responsibility for my well-being, I traded in my old glasses (self-pity) for a new pair (self-empowerment). Complaining about everything and being critical about other people was a lifestyle of the past, but today, I have so much more fun flushing down my old attitudes and making room for new adventures. Think about it. This can be your choice, too. ❧

Did an angel fly over my head and sprinkle fairy dust to inspire me to become a phoenix? Maybe. But I would also like to thank the people who prayed for me—either for my sake or their own. Yes, miracles do happen. Today, I love being a rocking-awesome Self-Care Vigilante on this magnificent planet and truly appreciate the incredible power of the human body. It is an honor to have one, learn from it, and partner with its power. Feeling vibrant is a definite treasure, and my new addiction to smiling and laughing offers me great energy to care for myself and serve others! ○≋

# Ingredient 3:

## RELEASE AND FLOW
*Rise Above Obstacles, Eliminate Toxins and Irritating Foods, and Release Mental and Emotional Triggers*

It may come as no surprise to you that I have written many journal entries that demonstrated my mastery in the art of emotional vomiting. My frustration, anger, and strife produced fantastic fertilizer for a garden that was destined to blossom from continuous showering of colorful four-letter words— most of which began with "F's" and "Sh's." Lots of fudge and sugar went into that garden. I am not completely cured of that, yet; however, many folks have noticed the significant progress. These days my favorite four-letter word that begins with the letter "F" is *F.L.O.W.*—*Feel Light Offering Wisdom.* Although I have mentioned this acronym before, I really enjoy saying it and think it is worth repeating.

Maintaining a healthy flow of energy, blood, breath, and nutrients *within* me stimulates favorable movement *around* me. I encourage the flow of goodies inside my body and delight in witnessing amazing feats throughout each day.

Emotional constipation, analysis paralysis, procrastination, and pessimism all did me a great favor. If it were not for these heavy thoughts in my darkness and despair, I would not have become so thirsty for grace, ease, and laughter. I do feel personally responsible for shaking loose and eliminating waste and toxins from my cells—literally and metaphorically. Even though I am not a doctor (but I'd like to play one on TV), my accumulation of a wealth of experience in addressing so many conditions helps me see that gold nuggets are everywhere, if you look. To get stronger I had to drop my misperceptions—or wave goodbye to old feelings of not being good enough, doing enough, or having enough. *BLAH!* ❦

This *not enough-ism* had to go!!! (Dear editor, may I use three exclamation points here?) My sense of not enough-ism was a living, thriving lie for so many years. It spawned many of my extreme actions and reactions, such as compulsive spending, overeating, masturbation, time-debting, and so much more. I subconsciously believed that there was never enough time, love, money, food, sex, etc., even when time, food, love, money, and feelings of satisfaction actually *were* within my reach. Despite my stomach and wallet being full, I was still hungry and could not buy enough of anything to satisfy me.

Addiction goes far beyond what is in the streets. When a *thousand* of something does NOT seem to be enough to satisfy you, then your taking *just one* could be too many—like pulling the pin out of a grenade—*BOOM!* The original expression is even more powerful: "...one is too many and a thousand is never enough" (from *Narcotics Anonymous, NA's* "Basic Text," page 18).

Dissatisfaction and disappointment ran very deep within me. These were seeds for a lifetime of discontent. For example, no matter how good I looked, my outsides never matched the mental image of the male body I should have had. I discovered that not enough-ism was not a cure for chronic pain but a primary ingredient in my soup of misery and hopelessness. To gain relief and joy and fulfill my mission on Earth, I had to take this huge and heavy pot off the stove. ✿

Shedding this sense of lack, or *scarcity consciousness*, rocketed me to new levels of growth, faith, and optimism after each challenging health crisis. Many generations of family had passed on to me their scarcity thinking. Efforts to save money did help them to survive wars and migration but crippled their health and vitality. I witnessed how their depriving themselves of quality food and medicine made them sick. Breaking this cycle, I make emotionally sober financial decisions, like spending money on personal care, investing in myself for a healthy future, and building creative projects to honor my God-given gifts. Bills and invoices will always arrive, but I find hope from every direction and respond with gratitude for the blessings received. Plenty of goodies have been here for and within me all along. It feels so good to be awake! ❧

To rise above obstacles, I adopted the habit of not blaming others for my problems. Had I continued holding grudges against every person who misdiagnosed, miscalculated, or misunderstood my medical conditions, I would not be enjoying the body I have today. Gone are the days when I pointed my finger at people who misread my injuries, took x-rays of wrong body parts, doubted my pain, limited my treatment options, or told me there was no cure. Continuing the blame game would have robbed my body of the vital energy and time for healing. Muscular strength, balance, and endurance need the support of a strong immune system.

In addition to eliminating toxins and waste by eating cruciferous vegetables, superfoods, and other goodies, I had to minimize the production of stress toxins created inside of me. A body full of anger, adrenaline, cortisol, and stuck energy has little chance of returning to homeostasis—a state of balance and comfort—and no chance of attaining higher levels of vibrancy. Had I held onto any resentment toward these doctors, negative energy and low vibrational frequencies ("bad vibes") would have flooded my body. Thinking, sounding, or behaving like a victim would have left me lying in the fetal position and accumulating chemical toxins produced by my very own body. That would *not* have been recovery. ❧

It took a lot of work for me to forgive what I perceived as physician incompetence and lack of compassion. I first began praying for their children, spouses, and parents before I could bring myself to wish wonderful blessings on those who contributed to my misery. Over time, information came to me that they were also struggling within themselves. They may have wanted to fix me, but were unable to do so for whatever reason. Healthcare and mental health professionals have their own battles with illness, compulsions, and other challenges, like anyone else.

My newfound perspective on physicians and other healthcare or mental health professionals inspired growth and compassion from within me. Freedom from any previous disappointment in them became priceless to me. I began to see doctors as souls in human bodies. First and foremost, they were human beings. Medical professionals are their own toughest critics; they have very high expectations of themselves to achieve perfect performance and complete knowledge—practically beyond human and almost God-like. Many view their options as limited, as years of education and training forced them to tolerate countless hours of sleep deprivation, malnourishment, and sacrificed relationships. This shows in their faces and bodies while they try to hide their aches, pains, and addictions.

Even with the technological advances of today, many have yet to enjoy a work/life balance that includes a promising career, quality time with life partners, and the joy of raising children and of caring for elderly parents. Practicing a robust self-care regimen may help them get to where they would like to be and offer them hope for a healthier future: physically, spiritually, and financially. They, their loved ones, and their patients would all benefit. What a wonderful win-win-win situation! ☙

With mental clarity, keen intuition, and bodies free of toxins, we are better prepared to face and overcome challenges that arise throughout the day. It is true that we cannot always prevent contaminated air, water, or food entering our bodies, but we can be proactive with graduated levels of precaution. Using portable air cleaners, water filters, and natural cleaning detergents (vinegar, baking soda, and rubbing alcohol) would be a good starting place.

Helping our bodies stay strong and getting rid of what does not belong in them is a personal journey that is different for everyone. There are many well-meaning people and wellness products and foods on the market, but finding what works for each of us requires courage to turn inward and make decisions based on our own body's response to medications, foods, chemicals, vitamins, powders, drops, pellets, injections, teas, and other substances.

How was I to make my body happy for the long run, with so many options to choose from in the marketplace? Where could I begin to address the symptoms of ailments in different parts of my body? Which experts should I listen to or follow? Facing the seemingly insurmountable task of sorting through which medications, vitamin supplements, foods, and drinks would make my body happy in the long run was not easy for me at the beginning. Rest assured, I was not the only one in that boat. The danger of generalizations about "the most effective way" or "the best method" for any condition is not the variety of solutions offered but the presumptuous way individuals, organizations, and businesses have declared that they know exactly what our bodies need. Hogwash.

Certain foods, products, and activities have worked well for me in my recovery and may (or may not) serve your needs, such as:

- Drinking warm-to-hot water before and after stretching (to flush and massage my internal organs)
- Eating parsley and cilantro (to release some unwanted metals)
- Enjoying kale, blueberries, and cabbage (to clean out gunk and replenish with goodies)
- Taking green juice and vitamins C, $D_3$, and $K_2$ (to strengthen my immune system and mental health)
- Using saline water for nasal irrigation (to keep my sinuses and head happy)
- Swallowing L-glutamine powder (for muscle recovery and healing digestive walls)
- And many other things ೞ

Remember: certain things help me at certain times, but it is my job to listen for what, when, and how much my body needs. This is your job as well. What serves me well could help you, too, but maybe only some of the time. To feel better than you do at this moment, you need to explore and listen to your body for what is appropriate for you.

Same story for the types of generic advice medical journals, health and fitness magazines, and television broadcasts offer the public. In general, magazines will tell you that drinking a lot of water helps to replenish our bodies; however, many seniors who are unable to retain sufficient sodium levels in their blood—highly critical for brain health—would benefit from drinking less plain water and would better replenish their bodies with beverages containing sodium, potassium, and electrolytes to minimize the light-headedness that may cause loss of balance and falling. And some medical researchers now believe that measuring the ratio of good to bad cholesterol (HDL:LDL) is not an absolute, reliable measure for preventing or monitoring heart disease, contrary to what journals have said for years. ❧

There are so many discussions on the precise combination of "diet and exercise" that would be the solution for "being overweight." If they worked across the board—and if everyone followed that advice—then our country would be quite lean and fit by now, which is not the case. From my personal experience and in working with others, I have discovered that most people lose physical strength and retain excess body fat when their internal organs and systems are unhappy. What makes a real difference is putting effort into improving the conditions of internal organs and providing ongoing support for efficient system functioning. When people become truly healthier and happier—with a greater sense of purpose and enjoyment in living—the issue of weight no longer dominates the conversation.

How the body metabolizes food (changes it into a form it can use) makes a huge difference. Give your body what it needs in doses it can handle. When I got healthier, I felt lighter. The pounds melted away—not because I went on a diet or exercised but because my internal organs got healthier and became happier. Plus I devoted time to releasing mental clutter, an overextended sense of responsibility, and remorse over lost time, opportunities, and people. I had to rise above any real or perceived obstacles and emotional discomfort caused by single or repeated negative events during my early childhood, especially those that reflected the trauma my parents and grandparents had experienced. ○3

Stepping out of the grave, so to speak, allowed me to shed the suitcases filled with hand-me-down beliefs and detach from burdens that did not belong in my cardiovascular (heart), pulmonary (lung), and digestive systems (from mouth to colon). I truly was on a path to win the battle against stress and developed the term *robusticity*—a combination of "robustness" and "elasticity." Just the thought of feeling robust and flexible at the same time excited me and still excites me now. Having emotional robusticity and great gut intuition continues to help me sort through mountains of information, foods, and products. My efforts have ignited new vigor for creating a peaceful home, enjoying fun people around me, and being a kid again, filled with a spirit of wonder and adventure! ♋

A Self-Care Vigilante, I strive to maintain a conscious connection with the Universe as my partner, a partner that supports and lifts me up at any given moment. Dialed into my intuition, I am able to improve the flow of blood, breath, and nutrients and the elimination of waste and toxins from my body, while minimizing stress through simple but powerful actions. Through tapping on meridian points of my energy superhighway, I support my nervous system in reversing muscle atrophy and regaining power in my legs. When I keep my internal organs happy, I attract people who also nourish their body, mind, and spirit. Today, I continue to stretch, improve my posture, and stimulate healthy growth in my bones, joints, and muscles.

Although it took years to recover muscle memory in my right leg and walk with balance, stability, and precision again, every step in my journey was like winning an Olympic gold medal. Despite many roadblocks and setbacks, my blessings were plentiful, especially when I focused on what I had and not what I lacked. One pleasantly surprising result was that I became a person who attracted brilliant, amazingly open-minded, and proactive physicians ("white coats," M.D.s, and D.O.s). They began to enrich my life and propel me forward. This was only the beginning. ♋

# Exercise for Chapter Seven

*Ilana's Mindfulness Meditation and Tapping Exercise for EMBRACING CHANGE in a 5-Part Format (adapted Progressive Energy Field Tapping or Pro EFT\*)*

Below are passages you may reflect on as you breathe deeply (**ॐ**) in silent meditation or say the words aloud while relaxing and tapping together the SIDES of both palms of your hands—the "karate chop point" (KC Point). *(See APPENDIX A: Tapping Meridian Points.)*

Please remember to drink some water before, during, and after this exercise.

❖ Reversal 1: "Even though my hesitation and uncertainty about making changes in my life holds me back from celebrating the positive results I want, there is a part of me that doesn't want to let it go—for whatever reason, logical or illogical. (Maybe I'm allergic to change or believe things get better when I do nothing.) But I want to love and accept myself anyway." **ॐ**

❖ Reversal 2: "Even though my doubts (push-and-pull battles) about whether or not I really need to change are driving me nuts and blocking me from enjoying vibrancy and confidence I desire, there is a part of me that still loves the drama and doesn't want to let it go. But I want to love, accept, and honor myself anyway." ❧

❖ Reversal 3: "Even though my wish for a magic wand to wave my problems away is keeping me from taking action and feeling good about myself, there is a part of me that is willing to wake up and do the next right thing. I want that part to win, because I love and accept myself." ❧

❖ Reversal 4: "Even though this remaining doubt about change being truly worthwhile holds me back from desirable progress, I choose to breathe deeply into my gut, borrow courage from the Universe, and surround myself with supportive role models. I love and accept myself deeply and completely." ❧

❖ CHOICE Statement: "I choose to take bite-sized steps to feed my body, mind, and spirit whatever makes them glad to be alive, so that I may rise up from the ashes like a phoenix and soar across the sky. And I deeply and completely love and accept myself." ❧

*Pro EFT™ (Progressive Energy Field Tapping™) and the process of reversal neutralization or "Reversal Setup" were developed by EFT Master Lindsay Kenny.

# CHAPTER EIGHT

# Next Three Ingredients

4. I accept love and support from an entire village of healthcare and healing professionals, family, friends, and neighbors.

5. I develop self-compassion for individual body parts, internal organs, and my entire being by creating time to heal and celebrating each bit of progress.

6. I live life on purpose and wholeheartedly embrace plenitude.

## Ingredient 4:

### UNITY AND PROXIMITY
*Accept Love and Support from an Entire Village*

I learned to accept love and support from an entire village of healthcare and healing professionals, family, friends, and neighbors. If you remember only one thing from this book, let it be this: *People*

*who allow others to love and support them in their*
*daily lives can get back on their feet—literally and*
*figuratively—sooner and smoother than those who*
*refuse help.* Because I had always preferred to be
and act on my own, I struggled with letting people
into my world. Fortunately, the Universe ignored
my protests and sent me a very understanding
community of friends, family, and neighbors. Many,
many strangers I had never met before became real
friends. It truly took an entire village to rebuild me.

For the record, I did not ask for this village.
Miss Independent was always fiercely self-sufficient
and very private. Despite having many friends in
12-step recovery, few people knew where I lived.
Even the neighbors on my block seldom saw me.
Jumping in my car and going elsewhere to see, meet,
or be of service to people, I was all over the map and
nowhere for long. When I lost my mobility, numerous friends disappeared. Seeing me in a wheelchair
most likely terrified them; I embodied the harsh
reality that they, too, could be disabled in a matter
of seconds. ↷

The Universe more than made up for the disap-
pearance of these individuals. Sincere, loving, and
dedicated people flooded into my life. I began to
believe that although I had made mistakes in the
past, I must have done something good for someone. Into my world came great healthcare providers
of traditional Western Medicine, alternative healing practitioners, therapists, spiritual leaders, family members, new friends, neighbors, chronic-pain

support groups, additional 12-step recovery fellowships, and yes, Red Sox Nation—the passionate, die-hard, international fan base of Boston's professional baseball team. Having tasted life's downs and ups of misery and victory, these people chose to share their time, talent, and wisdom with me. And I am paying it forward.

Have you seen my photo? I do not look like *Humpty Dumpty,* the giant egg from the children's fairytale who sat on a brick wall, but both he and I "had a great fall." However, I was the lucky one. "All the king's horses and all the king's men" *were* able to put me back together again—for the most part. My bones healed, but the tendons, ligaments, and soft tissue took much longer. During all this, something strange happened to my nervous system. My leg needed manual stimulation to help the blood flow through it, and the cells seemed to have forgotten how to absorb fresh oxygen and release carbon dioxide waste. My foot turned dark maroon-black and the muscles of my leg melted away, leaving only bones and very thin skin. ☙

Learning how to stop my right leg from dying before my very eyes demanded that I arrive at a deeper level of humility. Prior to this I had never even thought about changing the way my conscious mind processed information to support my autonomic nervous system, nor did I have the patience to do this. Many amazing people in my life showed me that it was possible. Although I thought many of their ideas were crazy, I was grateful to have followed them anyway. Being humble and accepting help created the life I have today. Eventually, all of these experiences offered me opportunities to share inspiration and hope with others facing the complex package of chronic pain, illness, and addiction.

In case you were wondering, I did not wake up one day and decide to use a trillion different strategies or methods to heal my body. My brain could never have scripted such an ingenious scenario, which is why I continuously give thanks to the Universe, Great Spirit, Source, or God for filling my world with such fantastic people. Now with my resilient legs, robust immune and nervous systems, and fully healed esophagus and vocal cords (whew!), I enjoy the fruits of our collaborative effort. Take a peek at the *partial* list of medical specialties, strategies, modalities, programs, techniques, and tools I have used thus far:

> *Internal medicine, orthopedic medicine, podiatry, neurology, pain management and rehabilitation, specialty ear/nose/throat, prescription medication, physical and aqua therapy, psychotherapy, psychiatry, cognitive behavioral modification for chronic pain, personal training, functional restoration program, somatic (musculoskeletal) therapy, neuromuscular massage therapy, chronotherapy, naturopathic medicine, homeopathic remedies, nutritional strategies, craniosacral therapy, Chinese medicine and herbs, acupuncture, Chi/ Qi Gong, meridian tapping, 12-step addiction*

*recovery programs, applied kinesiology, reiki, theta healing, mindfulness meditation, and a bit of yoga* ✂

My point in sharing this partial list is to say that no one person had everything I needed. The Universe understood the power of helping me see ways in which I was meant to connect with every individual I met along the way. This journey to rebuild my body was not about which school of thought was the best or which of the strategies, programs, and tools were most effective. What I began to see was that each person, process, and outcome further deepened my understanding of Universal Laws. Most importantly, the Universe consistently showed me that my allowing people to guide me was a clear demonstration of compassion for myself and for others. I unknowingly made life on Earth sweeter—no matter how challenging or unpleasant the situation. How about that?

During my visit on this planet, I have developed an appreciation for contrast in the presence of light and dark (Universal Law of Polarity), the power of accepting help wholeheartedly (Universal Law of Allowance), the possibility of feeling satiated or satisfied in a world of unlimited internal and external resources (Universal Law of Sufficiency and Abundance), the dynamics of positive and negative energy flow (Universal Law of Attraction and Repulsion), the benefits of joining a community of like-minded people (Universal Law of Proximity), and so much more.

Although many doctors were not able to treat my CRPS, somewhere in my body I was sure there were doctors who could. Carrying that vibration within me, I found "white coats" who were well established and secure enough in themselves enough to discuss treatment modalities beyond the scope of their specialty.

When I met my current physical medicine and rehabilitation (PM&R) specialist I first had to pass a drug test, because she cared whether or not I had any narcotics in my system. We pursued treatment options that kept prescription medication to a minimum. She referred me to a functional restoration program (FRP) where I learned new nutritional combinations, mindfulness meditation practices, relationship-building and boundary-setting techniques, and physical rehabilitation regimens that increased my ability to bathe and dress myself, as well as perform many other basic tasks. Today, she still makes suggestions that expand my toolbox and widen my exposure to the world—laughing and crying with me every step of the way.

While closely monitoring my migraine headaches, hypersensitivity to light, and sleep issues, my neurologist encouraged me to take my meditation practices to new heights. He guided me through *chronotherapy* to reset my body clock (circadian rhythm) to help improve my level of functioning during daylight hours. We did this while honoring my nocturnal high-creativity cycles. I probably will always be a real night owl, having astounding mental clarity without caffeine or sugar, but it really is nice to be able to enjoy mornings now.

Readjusting my sleep schedule with a combination of traditional and nontraditional support has produced positive results in my physical recovery and hope for the future. My neurologist inspired the idea of publishing this book as a Kindle eBook (in addition to paperback), as he continued to monitor my health for potential migraine headaches, carpal tunnel flare ups, and sleep issues throughout the entire period of writing and publishing what you now see before you. At his request for a guided meditation in this book, I included one at the end of Chapter Nine. You can experience the deep-breathing exercise I do every day to reaffirm my personal mantra of crossing finish lines with grace, ease, and laughter. ☙

My entire attitude toward time and ways to manage it shifted through my work with this neurologist. Did my deepened commitment to meditation open portals that granted me inner peace about managing time? Or did my newfound ability to live among day birds with the wisdom of a night owl further align me with Father Time? Maybe both. I look forward to sharing more on this discussion with you in Book 2. Stay tuned!

How very fortunate I am to have an internist who is also a licensed psychiatrist. She sees the entire picture of my health—mental as well as physical—and carefully looks at all the pieces that contribute to issues that flare up and reveal possible patterns. Still practicing within the traditional

Western Medicine model, my internist is open to discussing less conventional topics, such as the impact of environmental biology and of epigenetic factors upon our health, as explained by cell biologist Bruce Lipton, author of *The Biology of Belief.* She acknowledges that my health conditions stem not only from my family's medical history of disease but also the environmental factors and trauma that affected them. I did inherit my parents' traits (eye color, hair, etc.). However, along with the genes (DNA) I received some of the byproducts of environmental exposure to natural and synthetic elements, chemicals, political instability, war, cultural strife, personal traumatic experiences, and so on. ☙

The good news is that despite the not-so-nice trauma in my ancestors' genetic makeup, we *can* influence how our genes express themselves. Our life experiences can shape the condition of our bodies and the DNA structure within each cell. I like using pizza and calzone to explain. If I were to put a fresh, hot pizza in the backseat of my car and then suddenly step on the brakes, the pizza box would fly off the seat and onto the floor. The pizza itself could fold over and look somewhat like a giant calzone. It is the same pizza with the same ingredients (genes), but it now appears different (structural change). The calzone-looking pizza now produces a different eating experience, as the person bites into a lot more crust, first, and then tastes the cheese and tomato sauce. No one added more crust, but the experience changed.

Both of my parents grew up in war-torn nations, affecting what and how they ate, worked, accumulated possessions, viewed themselves and others, and gave birth and raised me. I still have many of the physical features of my ancestors, but more interestingly, my internal organs have manifested the trauma they experienced. For example, chronic asthma attacks throughout my childhood were not coincidental. Neither parents had these symptoms. However, in my lungs I embodied the combination of sadness and separation anxiety they experienced when having to flee multiple homes in their mother country to escape death. ❃

My sense is that the low vibrational frequency that I inherited in my lungs contributed to low-vibe behavior, like smoking. I exacerbated my asthmatic lungs—dying faster by the minute from smoking cigarettes and marijuana, neither of which I have touched since 1995 and 2000, respectively. I take full responsibility for all my old damaging behavior but realize that the stuck energy was here before I even arrived on this planet.

My job is to flush out what I can, make amends to my body parts, and bless everyone with the person I am now. Today, my posture is beautiful, and I feel so much lighter. Freedom is truly exciting and gets even better when we release ourselves from inherited trauma and limiting beliefs by using tapping, Chi Gong, prayer, meditation, and exercise, for example. With rejuvenated willingness to be on this planet, I stretch throughout the day—especially my arms, neck, shoulders, and chest muscles—to make more room for my ribcage and lungs to expand and perform the best they can.

We all have a "right now" with which we can make living amends to our bodies and let go of the burden (stuck energy) that has been weighing us down, whether we consciously know it or not. This is how we step into our real shoes—not hand-me-down shoes that were made for other people—and reclaim our lives with permission to move forward and thrive.

Deeply grateful I am for everyone who has stepped onto my path of recovery, including those who were willing and able to offer helpful solutions, as well as those who were not ready to stretch beyond their comfort zones. I now have a keen intuitive sense about who can teach me more and help me progress in attaining higher levels of recovery. I take action steps to invite people to support my journey and allow the Universe to line them up according to its timeline. Honoring the Universal Law of Proximity, I deliberately surround myself with beings that glow, heal, and cherish their visit on planet Earth and want to make the most of it. Join me as I continue on this bridge that connects traditional Western Medicine with Eastern wisdom. We are One. ೞ

# Ingredient 5:

## SELF-COMPASSION AND TIME-ABUNDANCE CONSCIOUSNESS
*Develop Self-Compassion and Create Time to Heal and Celebrate*

### SELF-COMPASSION

I believe that having compassion for oneself and others makes this world a better place. When I am hungry but do not eat, thirsty but do not drink water, tired but do not take a break, you would not want to be anywhere near me—trust me on that. Try relaxing around me when I am beating myself up for being perfectly imperfect. Observe the effects of all the above: unhappy internal organs, a sour-looking face, and emotional vomiting that would not be music to anyone's ears.

One of the key ingredients for creating vibrancy, inside and out, is self-compassion. It was a learning process, but I discovered that actively thanking and cherishing each and every individual part and internal organ produced favorable results. Evidence of self-compassion appears in many forms. Look at someone and ask yourself if this person looks as if he or she consciously appreciates having a body, a nose, maybe arms and legs. Does he periodically replenish himself with water or non-caffeinated tea? Does her body look comfortable the way she stands, sits, and walks? These questions and more greatly reveal whether or not we are wearing shoes that help support our balance, using the bathroom when we need it, and exercising healthy boundaries to feel safe and happy around people.

I have not always understood the importance of self-compassion and time for healing. My mind declared itself to be far superior to my body and thereby ignored it. That mind was wrong, of course. Changing the language in the thoughts between my ears was critical to recovery. But more importantly, the brain *of my body* needed to be heard. For example, I have always loved to eat, even when I was full. That caused problems—big ones. My stop button was broken. No fat-burning teas, powders, or weight-loss programs could remove the childhood scars from my having been bullied and from suffering from decades of low self-esteem, guilt, shame, and embarrassment. Quick fixes do not resolve chronic conditions. Just ask people with diabetes who cannot quit sugar. ∝

To truly recover at the cellular level, I had to let my mind take the back seat so that my body could heal the damaged nerves and cells that stored remaining trauma. The concept and practice of offering myself compassion through everyday self-talk and action was critical to creating new neuro-pathways that led to my walking again. I accidentally discovered that I could restore my legs by singing to my toes. You heard me: I sang to my toes.

## Story of the Stranger and His Foot

One very hot summer day in 2007, a friend drove me to the store to purchase a portable air conditioner.

At that time, my progressive condition was in only one of my legs. However, I clenched my teeth like a tough guy and braced myself against the painful vibration I felt through the car floor and seats. It was all worth it, because the Universe sent me an angel on that very afternoon.

After I made the purchase, my friend went to get her car while I waited outside the store entrance. Suddenly, I noticed a man standing about twenty feet away. Upon seeing me look at him, he nodded his head toward my leg and asked me to describe my pain. What a kindred spirit! Rather than inquiring as to what had happened like most people did, he showed concern for how I was feeling at that very moment.

Words did not come out well (brain fog), but my face spoke volumes. He began to tell me, "My foot turned black, too. I lost my muscles like your leg." I sat stunned in my wheelchair. He was so bold to talk about a foot I could barely look at. "Your foot is ice-cold in this crazy heat, and you can't find a comfortable position to get any relief," he stated. I nodded—still no words.

He continued, "First, my toes went black and the doctors cut them off. But then, this part went black," as he pointed to the middle part of his shoe. "They cut off more of my foot, but the rest of it kept dying. So they cut all of it up to here." He indicated the area above his ankle where they had amputated his entire foot. "The worst part of it all is that my foot's gone, but the pain still takes my breath away!" he declared and shook his head. They had replaced his foot with a mechanical one, but the phantom pain remained. ☙

As my friend pushed my wheelchair to the car, I waved to the man and uttered a few words of appreciation. His concern and depth of understanding profoundly touched me. Suddenly, he shouted these last words to me, "Don't let them take your foot! Save it! Don't let them take your foot!"

I still vividly remember how clumsily I climbed into my friend's car. The man's last words continued to echo in my head. What a daze! No one had ever expressed so clearly how I was feeling or what was truly happening to me. This man was different. Although his tone of voice was pretty matter-of-fact during most of the conversation, it was his intense and passionate battle cry that moved mountains. **Right then and there, I declared to my friend that I would go to any lengths to keep my foot and heal my leg. Although clueless and powerless over this dastardly disease, I was on a mission to save my foot.**

The very next morning, I heard a cute little tune in my head and began singing it in a whisper, "I love my toes, and my toes love me. I love my foot, and my foot's a part of me." Pause, honor, and cherish. Then I belted, "I love my leg—it's amazing! I love my toes, and my toes love me." ☙

I have sung this tune over and over every single morning to my toes, feet, and legs since that hot summer's day in 2007. Even when I lost my voice in 2011, I sang it in my mind while lovingly touching my toes with my fingers on a "good day" and with my eyes on a "not-so-good day." This is still a vital part of my daily regimen in preparing my body for each day. I tell my toes that I will never give up on helping blood to flow through them. Every cell in my toes, feet, and legs will receive fresh oxygen and easily release carbon dioxide and anything else it no longer needs. ⚞

The stranger who pleaded with me, "Don't let them take your foot!" was my guardian angel. He ignited my journey into body-part reconciliation. I began to look at, think about, touch, and embrace my toes, feet, and legs with interest, love, and compassion, like never before. To save my foot, I showered both feet with love. I no longer saw my foot as a liability or something that had disappointed and betrayed me. Instead, I became its biggest cheerleader, filling it with hope, approval, and a sense of belonging.

**This is the foundation of Body-Part Reconciliation™ (BPR), an ongoing process of making living amends to injured, abused, or neglected parts of the body. Fed with vibrant energy and appreciation, their cells may find new life. The goal is to feel and express compassion for every part of the entire body and enjoy higher vibrational frequencies emerging from that expression. Let us cherish all that we do have and celebrate every inch of it! ⚞**

Before CRPS, my feet had taken me on countless great adventures. They helped me to climb to the top of the Mohave Desert's Eureka Dunes, ski down black-diamond mountain trails in New England, walk on ancient soil in the jungles of Borneo, dance salsa until dawn in the streets of New York, and much, much more. After the arrival of CRPS, it became *my* turn to carry my feet, and I began to do exactly that—cherish and honor every inch of them with patience and gratitude for their company. ৫৪

## TIME-ABUNDANCE CONSCIOUSNESS

Training my brain to stay out of the way of my body's restoration process was quite a tug-of-war. I wanted to give my body a short amount of time to do its repair work and then move forward with my life. It seemed reasonable to me, as I had already lost time dealing with my injuries. However, demanding that my body respond to my intellectual commands was pointless. On top of that, I was wasting energy and time trying to control everything that could not be controlled—pain, doctors, the clock, broken bones, torn soft tissue, nervous systems—multiple factors woven together.

While meditating one day I heard, "Time is on my side. Take opportunities to shape it for keeping my body safe and calm through everything." With this I allowed my body to do what it knew best, and it began to heal.

I used to live in time-scarcity consciousness, believing that there was never enough time for anything. Rushing around all over town, I always felt behind in the race against time. Plaguing me was the false idea that my ability to multi-task—doing several things at the same time—meant that I was a super-productive person. Au contraire! Like a true drama queen, I even enjoyed the status of being an *overachiever* and chose not to accept the reality that multi-tasking added burden to my nervous system and created traffic jams in my brain. Constantly shifting mental gears, I did not give neuro-pathways, carrying all sorts of messages to different parts of the body, the appropriate chance to deliver messages to their destinations. Too many messages were deemed *top priority*; I forced my body to deal with countless traffic collisions that caused even more crashes. Get the picture?

I was a *pro* at burning out all my gears but somehow finding one more small reserve gear that I trusted to get me across the finish line. With high expectations of achievement, my mind was not about to let anyone down; feeling disappointed or disappointing anyone else was completely unacceptable. Overcompensating for every mistake or weakness left me exhausted as I spent time and energy back-tracking—undoing and redoing whatever my mind deemed necessary. This was how I fell even further behind in my personal race against time. The problem was that crossing many finish lines this way and forcing positive outcomes did not offer me long-lasting happiness or a sense of well-being on this planet. I was still behind—or so I thought. ❧

Thank goodness I do not see myself or treat myself this way any longer. Developing a completely different understanding of time was a must! Making friends (not enemies) with time brought me to a new level of vibrancy. In collaboration with the Universe, I consciously design periods of time throughout the day to reconnect with the mother ship for verifying my course and allowing her to download information I may need, while recharging my batteries. My laptop and cell phone work better when they are fully charged. So do I. ☙

Note that I still have 24 hours in a day like before. But now I shape (not make) time so that I may flow through the day with grace, ease, and laughter—especially laughter. **Shaping time to decompress and re-energize on a regular basis, I restore my ability to focus and be productive for whatever else the Universe has in store for me.** In my daily calendar are numerous short periods to rest and stretch my vessel with deep breathing and body centering exercises. Clearing my thoughts and expanding my heart, I invite wisdom, power, and light to support me in functioning more optimally at all levels, internally and externally. This is a very loving action step, not only for myself *now* but also for *future me.* It honors space for rejuvenation so that I can be of greater service to others. Today, I can shout from any mountaintop, "Resting is investing!" You heard me: "Resting is investing."

**There is plenty of time for everything the Universe needs me to do.** My body could not have gained an ounce of quality recovery had I not made peace with time. My first few years in bed and in a wheelchair were brutal because of my unhealthy relationship with time. Staying home was a prison sentence, and I had to retrain my brain to treat this time with respect and care, no matter how bad my physical pain was.

All my personal flaws, character defects, and shadows rose to the surface. Symptoms of hyperactivity disorder and other compulsive tendencies flared up and filled my mind with horrible thoughts. I watched dust bunnies grow and multiply, saw bacteria spread everywhere in my mind's eye, and nearly collapsed from the frustration of not being able to clean my own house. What I eventually discovered was that the more I struggled, the more I needed to focus on what was happening *inside* my body. ଔ

Even though I was too hyper to meditate much, meditation became the primary tool of relief from my insanity. Nursing my injuries, I gave every ounce of energy I had to reconnect my body, keep my nose in the AA "12 x 12," and coach the Red Sox (via computer screen) which—as you probably well know—led to their winning the World Series on the day before my fourth AA birthday. This gift alone was far sweeter than any honey, baklava, or honey-soaked baklava I have ever kissed. If you still do not think meditation can lead you to progress, give it a chance to open great doors for you anyway.

The Universe was very generous in sending me the wisdom to slow down, stop, breathe deeply, and rebuild—not just physically, but mentally. The wiser part of me realized that the act of resting created an investment in my future. From my wheelchair I watched people run around like chickens without a GPS. Arrogantly, I thought, "I'll never be like them again. They have no idea how silly they look!" This was easy for me to say, as I was confined and limited by my body.

The true test of a changed mindset revealed itself after I was able to walk again. To remind myself of my new resolve, I developed this personal mantra: "I choose to pace myself gently, like a marathon runner, so that I may glide across the finish line in all areas of my life with grace, ease, and laughter." With this mantra's energy flowing throughout my body, I do not have to end up being a chicken sans GPS. ❧

My time-abundance mindset expanded as I concentrated more and more on breathing deeply, meditating on beautiful images, and visualizing peaceful, easy-flowing energy everywhere. Soon, I was able to see that people who were busy all the time were not necessarily healthy or fun to be around. This inspired me to reflect upon how I used to fill my calendar with activities—confirmation that I was valuable and needed. Receiving external validation fed me a false sense of well-being and comfort, justifying my existence on this planet. The fallacy had to end. And thankfully, it did.

Putting the time, energy, and love into rebuilding my body, reconnecting my heart, and clearing my mind has evolved into a great long-term investment. **I enjoy a state of continuous gratitude that no amount of money can buy and celebrate each bit of success along the way.** All these efforts to relax, connect, and heal were highly rewarding. Even when I appeared to be sliding backward in physical strength and endurance, I actually was moving forward and up to the next level. As strange as it may sound, it is possible to feel totally crappy and still make progress at the very same time. A caterpillar sleeps in a cocoon before emerging as a butterfly. This can happen for humans as well. ⚓

Embracing this mindset that I have plenty of time to do everything necessary—according to the Universe—has freed me from decades of time-debting, regrets, and self-battery. I share more deeply this priceless transformation in Book 2 of the series, for it has exponentially changed my life for the better—health-wise, in my relationships with people, money, and myself. Embracing Mother Earth and Father Time, I have blossomed with a wonderful new sense of purpose! ⚓

## Ingredient 6:

### PURPOSE AND PLENITUDE
*Live Life on Purpose and Embrace That There Is Plenty*

Whenever unsure about a decision or path to take, I ask the question, "Where does the Universe need me?" This is a very powerful question I use that prompts the Universe to offer me guidance. Sometimes, I add, "...and please make it obvious!" Where I am supposed to be may reveal whom I will serve and what I will be doing at any given point in time. The answers may not always come immediately, but asking the question opens doors that bring me into alignment with a source of amazing strength, creativity, and wisdom.

I am right where I am supposed to be. Serenity is comfort in knowing that I am safe, protected, and able to share my abilities from a place of joy and harmony. Unafraid of losing anything or anyone, I sense that whatever is removed from me will be replaced by something else that nourishes my soul. With each gift of desperation—physical, emotional, or financial—I can embrace opportunities to start from scratch and rebuild, always allowing my soul to breathe freely. ✃

**Today, my functional definition of having serenity is demonstrating through action or inaction that no matter where I am, I trust the Universe to provide me with the exact necessary ingredients to contribute another piece to a grand design for the greater good of all.** Countless blessings inspire me to continue shining in my brilliance and forego hiding, one breath at a time and one baby step at a time. I no longer spend time creating and crossing out long to-do lists, dwelling on the past, or fantasizing about the future. Today, I flow throughout my day with a sense of peace that I am where

I am supposed to be, doing what the Universe needs me to do.

Memories of the past occasionally flicker into my mind. However, 12-step recovery has taught me to look (not stare) at the past and learn from it. Stories of yesterday may reveal something to us, but enjoying the present moment is most precious. Setting intentions on how I would like my future to look creates good vibrations in my organs and healthy hormones, like endorphins, right at this moment. This, in turn, opens me up to flowing in even more goodies.

Richness in the future begins with living it today. Layer by layer, I continue to break away from my tunnel-vision lenses so that I may live in an expanded reality. An infinite supply of goodness is at my disposal. I dissolve my handcuffs and prison bars that no longer serve me and reach beyond money, gold, and status to experience limitless slices of heaven on Earth that have been inside me all along. You too can choose to emerge from your distractions and grant yourself permission to shine from the inside out. ⌘

I certainly did not always feel that the Universe knew what it was doing, especially when intolerable physical pain was my constant companion. My world became very, very small. However, it forced me to make an important life-altering decision. I could shrink into nothingness, or I could grab onto life with full gusto and passion. Gratefully, I found people and situations that were like mirrors for me: I could see myself in them. Somehow, they inspired me to live life with a sense of purpose and to believe that the Universe has an abundance of goodies for everyone—including *me*.

The Universe brought into my life beautiful, sensitive, big-hearted, and highly creative people who were unable to see these qualities in themselves. Feeling unworthy and undeserving, they kept themselves busy with all sorts of activities, lists, and tasks, while resisting opportunities to engage fully in exploring their talents, gifts, and adventures in this big world. Either consciously or subconsciously, they worked hard to remain unnoticed and as invisible as possible.

Slow was their suicide—using alcohol and other substances and depriving themselves of nutritious foods, fresh air, human touch, and sunlight. For whatever reason, they carried in their hearts and bodies the belief that they were a burden to their parents, spouses, children, friends, neighbors, or society. I saw their breaths were short, as if they had permission to consume only minimal amounts of air. They sat on only one side of a chair to avoid taking up too much space and were hesitant to speak their thoughts for fear of being heard, seen, or punished. Their bodies broke down and were left unheard, uncared for, and unloved. Believing that there was never enough food, time, or love, they kept themselves locked in a vicious cycle of guilt, shame, and disappointment. ଔ

The Universe revealed that what I saw in them was in me. I then clearly understood that letting go of self-deprivation and replacing it with self-compassion was a dire necessity if I wanted my body to heal as smoothly as possible. **Giving myself permission to breathe, heal, dream, expand, take action, and expand again—and to feel like a first-class passenger able to travel anywhere—has become my way of life.** My vision is to be of maximum usefulness with joy bubbles that come from within, as I cross finish lines to serve others with grace, ease, and laughter.

To do this, I had to break an old pattern of isolating myself, as it offered nothing but a false sense of safety and stability. Not engaging frequently with people might have spared me from some discomfort or danger, but it did not erase the heartache and trauma that had been smothering my body cells for years. Doing things alone did help me to avoid seeing character defects and shadows of myself in others, but it could not protect me from being a judge, jury, and executioner against me, myself, and I.

On top of this, my escape-artist days did not serve me well. Running from one quick-fix drug, food, hobby, or relationship to another pulled me away from the joy and security I was meant to have and diminished my sense of purpose on this planet. Then physical pain kept me focused exactly on that: pain. My world became very tiny, as I huddled in isolation to keep safe from a world that might bring me more pain. The worst part of it all was that I saw myself as useless, unable to help myself or anyone else. *DARN*—that hurt! ✑

I finally woke up to the reality that I was put here on Earth simply because I was supposed to exist and be here, for whatever reason, known or unknown. That still holds true today. I am plenty, have plenty, do plenty, and there is plenty of time. My job is to keep my mind, spirit, and body open to the human experience of beauty, safety, and connection with people, animals, and nature. Piecing together moments that make me glad to be here on this planet, I have many slices of heaven on Earth to form an entire pie. All my perceived troubles have been worthwhile. In the habit of focusing on what is positive, peaceful, and precious, I can see, attract, and produce exactly that. Amazing things happen!

Each one of us is a connector between the Universe above and Mother Earth beneath our feet. How powerful we are: just by thinking of sending light and energy from the crown of our heads to our feet, we are channeling energy between the soil below and the galaxies beyond. Serving as wonderful conduits of energy and love is enough to justify our existence, our reason for being here. I am here, and so are you. Simply, we are beautiful. ଔ

## Exercise for Chapter Eight

*Ilana's Mindfulness Meditation and Tapping
Exercise for PERMISSION TO SHINE in a 5-Part
Format (adapted Progressive Energy Field
Tapping or Pro EFT\*)*

Below are passages you may reflect on as you
breathe deeply (☚) in silent meditation or say the
words aloud while relaxing and tapping together
the SIDES of both palms of your hands—the "karate
chop point" (KC Point). *(See APPENDIX A: Tapping
Meridian Points.)*

Please remember to drink some water before,
during, and after this exercise.

❖   Reversal 1: "Even though my desire to hide,
remain isolated, and stay small prevents me
from feeling courageous and excited each day,
there's a part of me that doesn't want to let
it go and let me grow—for whatever reason,
logical or illogical—but I want to love and
accept myself anyway."☚

❖   Reversal 2: "Even though my insecurities about
people, places, and money hold me back from
feeling confident and grateful for my talents
and gifts, a part of me still thinks it's not safe to
trust anyone, but another part of me wants to
trust someone. I want to love and accept both
parts of me." ☚

❖ Reversal 3: "Even though a part of me still wants to be small and stay in my comfort zone, there is another part of me that wants to say 'Yes' to new opportunities and have courage to be of service to more people. I want that part to win, because I love and accept myself and value my talents and gifts." ☙

❖ Reversal 4: "Even though these remaining fears and insecurities hold me back from engaging with others and sharing my talents, I choose to access the Universe's strength, wisdom, and power to bring blessings to more people's lives, one baby step at a time. I love and accept myself unconditionally." ☙

❖ CHOICE Statement: "I choose to be grateful for all the good in my life and vibrate this wonderful energy into the world, living each moment with a strong sense of purpose to create slices of heaven on Earth. Now I grant myself permission to SHINE, because I deeply and completely love and accept myself always!"

*Pro EFT™ (Progressive Energy Field Tapping™) and the process of reversal neutralization or "Reversal Setup" were developed by EFT Master Lindsay Kenny.*

# CHAPTER NINE

# The Active Ingredient

## Self-Care Vigilante Consciousness

"We will intuitively know how to handle situations which used to baffle us" is one of my favorite passages from the "Big Book," page 84. What if your mind, body, and spirit could all agree on what, how much, and how often you should eat? What if all three could select exercises gentle enough to pull you out of pain yet rigorous enough to take you to the next level? What if you could trust your mind, body, and spirit to choose relationships that inspire greater personal growth and harmony in all your interactions?

To these "what if" questions I say, "Bring it on!" Following my intuition has led me to great relief, freedom, and confidence. I take action to sharpen my gut instincts on a daily basis. Clarity is yummy. Listening for what the Universe deems as the top priorities of each day keeps me flowing along smoothly. Having continuous conversations with my body, I boldly adopt new habits and solutions, while releasing fear, anxiety, and stress into Mother Earth, who so powerfully recycles them into vibrant energy. I embrace my gift for discovering how people, things, and events are interconnected; there are no coincidences. With exuberance I move forward to wherever the Universe places me and bring my magnificent team of mind, body, and spirit into the action. My very deep breaths channel what I need to know, expand my field of energy, and support me in bridging any situation before me. This is how I serve. ⚭

My having conversations with my body is not just for healing ("What do you need?") or entertainment ("You look a bit funny today!") purposes. I literally tap my body first to release whatever is inside me that it no longer needs to hold—like waste, toxins, stuck energy—and then shine a spotlight on what I can use to serve someone or a situation. All my efforts to stay fully present in the moment and connected to the Universe's unlimited resources have proven to be highly worthwhile. Unlike ever before, I take care of myself with great respect and reverence for my body, mind, and spirit as one entity—a sparkling star in the vast Universe beyond and within me. What a blessing to find people treating me this way as well. You heard it from me: Positive energy *is* remarkably contagious! ⚭

As you may remember, for decades my mind believed that it reigned superior over my body and acted as if it was fully capable of managing any situation, including repairing injuries and overcoming pain. However, that strategy brought me only temporary, fleeting comfort. In denial, I found willpower to be effective for about two-and-a-half seconds, like people who use common sense and willpower to stop smoking, drinking, or eating sugar. I was not able to stay stopped, and neither could they.

Facing chronic pain on top of everything else exhausted me immensely. To fight fires that flared up throughout my body, I tried many different prescription medications, but the side effects worsened my condition. *The puzzle got too com-pli-cated.* My brain hurt from thinking so much; *feeling overwhelmed* would be an understatement. Embracing insanity, I kept trying to use my mind to control pain until it crashed, over and over again. Eventually, I found life on this planet no longer appealing. ∞

Only after an amazing epiphany did I make any real progress: our bodies have minds of their own. This realization shattered my valiant but fragile ego. Bodies know what to do and when to repair whatever is necessary to regain strength, stability, and vitality. How jealous I became of my body's powerful brain! But after calming down I then understood. When doctors deliberately induce coma in patients, they are allowing their patients' bodies to heal without distractions from their conscious minds. Conserving energy for real work to be done is an absolutely brilliant concept. Leaving the conscious mind out of the process is even more brilliant.

Convincing my mind to take a step back and not interfere with the work of my body was no

easy task. It kept jumping in and bossing everyone around while disrupting my need for rest and
recuperation. My mind became even more domi-
neering and disrespectful whenever my body failed
to obey it and worked even harder in the attempt to
control everything. With an inferiority complex, my
mind became the neighborhood bully. If this sounds
like a lack of self-compassion to you, then we are on
the same page.

The opposite of self-compassion is self-abandonment. As Queen of Self-Abandonment (see
my photo in the dictionary)—one who enters and
remains in very dark places—I allowed social
demands and expectations to distract me from
listening to what my body was trying to tell me.
Fitness magazines, shows, and news programs
sought to educate me without knowing my medical
history and complexity. Strangely, what *they* said
had greater influence upon me than my very own
gut intuition. I focused on the well-being of family, friends, clients, and everyone else and starved
myself of rest and nutrients. This habit did not
serve me well, yet I was unable to stop. Compulsive
gift giving, under-earning, and martyrdom did
not improve my physical, financial, emotional, or
spiritual health. Demonstrating to others that their
comfort was more important than mine, I paid their
bills and searched for solutions to their problems.
I was completely unaware that my actions deprived
them of self-confidence and dignity gained from
finding their own way. ∞

We are the last ones to see it, but our loved ones also suffer when we neglect and abandon ourselves. I have known people who died from falling asleep at the wheel while driving home after working long hours. Surgeons have lost their steady hands while battling addictions and other chronic illnesses. Single parents have fallen physically and financially sick trying to be and do everything for everyone else but themselves.

Learning from other people's lessons might have saved me, but earning a master's degree from the school of hard nocks rocketed me to where I am now. From darkness into light, my spirit finally was able soar!

## The Choice of Self-Investment

My cornucopia of illnesses was a humungous gift from the Universe; it propelled me toward making the most important investment ever—a self-care lifestyle that puts time, money, and love into creating the best odds for a healthy future. With the assistance of countless individuals and their amazing tools, I made it through the many stages of loss and grief over my life before CRPS. From denial, shock, anger, sadness, shame, and embarrassment, I rose out of the ashes to shine brilliantly, inside and out.

Becoming physically disabled in my late thirties gave me the opportunity to begin learning how to overcome challenges elderly people face in their later years. Today, I still have quite an arsenal of equipment and gadgets and know how to use them well. My previous and current physical limitations have inspired deep appreciation for adaptations to the toilet, clothing that makes getting dressed easier, gadgets for opening food and other types of packaging, a variety of walking accessories, safer solvents and methods for house cleaning, items for greater vehicle comfort, and so much more.

While acquiring all these goodies, I felt compelled to set a new goal for myself: to take care of my own bathroom needs for as long as possible—with grace, ease, and laughter. Running for U.S. President could be a more impressive goal, but I prefer the simpler things in life these days. Feeling vulnerable about being physically disabled inspired this. Still fresh in my mind are memories of having difficulty swallowing my saliva, climbing onto and off the toilet seat, and struggling to sit for twenty minutes. I aspire to be strong and healthy enough to do my private business in the bathroom without needing assistance from anyone for decades to come—pretty darn sexy, I will venture to say. ∞

Think about it: my dedication to self-care might be saving you from having to do these kinds of things for me. And *your* commitment to taking good care of yourself could bring much peace and happiness to everyone—me, you, *and* your loved ones. Imagine spending more time being creative, playing, and laughing. What a win-win-win situation!

## Self-Care Vigilante Mindset

I am a Self-Care Vigilante, and the payoff has been tremendous. Without tug-of-wars and endless arguments in my head, I am now free to flow through my day with grace, ease, and laughter. Everything I do is driven by my sincere desire to nourish all parts of me and let go of anything that does not.

Allow my gift of desperation to be an inspiration for your self-care. Do not wait until you lose your legs, hands, voice, or anything else to begin building a strong collaborative team of mind, body, and spirit. Develop compassion for yourself through self-care activities that help enjoy being in your body for as long as you are on this planet. Your future self will thank you for making this commitment. This is a freedom definitely worth fighting for—today and tomorrow.

In love with the wisdom of transforming pain into pleasure, I now aspire to shape tears into laughter. Through years of pain in the school of hard knocks, I developed this list of personal affirmations to keep my focus on gratitude, connection, and resilience. Every day, I weave these 26 *Self-Care Vigilante Affirmations* into all I do. May you find comfort, inspiration, and self-confidence as these statements become your reality!

**Affirmation 1, Love Every Part: "I love myself and every part of my body."** ෨

I embrace my vision of feeling safe and fantastic in my body and enjoying my life with gusto. To do so, I pay attention to any area of my body that calls for my respect, care, or special attention. No longer rejecting and judging any part of it for being in pain, I make living amends to my body parts with kind thoughts, kind words, and kind deeds. The sooner I help my blood flow smoothly, the more effectively my internal organs can function. With greater balance in male-female energy (yin-yang, respectively), my systems can work more efficiently.

Using an ancient Hawaiian prayer of reconciliation and forgiveness, *Ho'oponopono*—"I'm sorry. Please forgive me. Thank you. I love you."—as well as many other tools and techniques, I practice body-part reconciliation to release stuck energy induced by traumatic events, injury, neglect, overuse, or abuse. For example, I guide my feet to heal by saying "Hello my feet. I'm sorry that you are tired and hurting. Please forgive me for expecting too much from you today. Thank you for carrying me this far. I love you, my right foot and my left foot. So glad to have you both!"

Awake and aware, I acknowledge just how beautifully connected all parts of my body are to each other, as well as linked to every living being on this planet and beyond. My choice is to glow and flow! ✂

**Affirmation 2, Cleanse: "I feed my body and soul ingredients that cleanse anything that does not belong in me."** ℅

Little by little, I strengthen my skills in listening to what my body tells me it needs to absorb and release. My ongoing dialogue with my small intestine (the amazing brain) inspires a collaboration of my mind, body, and spirit. Holding both hands together with my palms facing upward as if to receive a bag of gold coins, I tap the sides of my hands at the "karate chop point" between the pinky finger and wrist joints. My small intestine loves responding to this very simple, natural way to inspire good decisions about what my body can and cannot use with each bite I take.

This is deliberate recovery in action—consciously connecting the brain between my ears and my super-intelligent small intestine so that they work together in delivering the necessary nutrients for building new healthy cells. I believe that the process of digesting food is highly spiritual and deserves my attention, respect, and gratitude. Taking deep breaths and tapping away negative thoughts and energy before touching any food can support healthy digestion. Then, chewing food thoroughly is critical in readily absorbing nutrients, and so, I developed the habit of not eating while I drive, talk on the phone, or watch television. Taking each bite is about reveling in abundance, which is everywhere. Paying attention to the little things truly means a lot.

My body occasionally asks me to make significant changes to what I eat, but as long as I pay attention to its signals, I am on the right track. Digestive enzymes have been very helpful at times; deep breathing has always increased impulse control; stretching exercises have improved my breathing, posture, and metabolism; and meridian tapping has enhanced the movement of blood, breath, nutrients, waste, and natural energy needed to make everything function optimally. The big payoff is that after eating, I always feel light and energetic yet calm and balanced at the same time. Having great internal plumbing feels fantastic—"Happy organs, happy life!"

**Affirmation 3, Laugh: "I laugh to 'pee-point' every single day." ❤**

I smile whenever people ask what inspired me to create this affirmation. Getting mad used to come very easily to me, but I now have a great habit of finding gratitude the very instant my blood begins to boil. Replacing any harsh words in my mind, I look for and grab onto astoundingly funny things to laugh about all day long. From this exercise I end up smiling most of the time, thanks to my focus on things that make my visit on this planet truly enjoyable. However, I do not stop there.

I love to laugh so hard that my face turns red, my jaw aches, and my bladder is about to burst. Laughing to pee-point is glorious. The search for the brighter side of everything is worth it. Although highly competent in finding things to complain about, I now prefer to ditch the heavy energy that no longer fits me. After laughing really hard, I feel lighter all the way around. And why not? My crazy nerve condition practically drives me to find something funny in *everything* so that I do not go out of my mind. That is why I am dead serious about laughing. Try laughing while peeing; it might be a fun adventure for you too. "Don't knock it until you've tried it," as they say.

"Laughter is the best medicine" is a great truth. Dosage, frequency, and delivery method are all highly relevant as well. I believe that a self-care regimen that expands our capacity to laugh deeply, frequently, and freely delivers the best medicine. A Self-Care Vigilante, I do laugh (and pee) often. "Congrats!" you say? Thank you very much.

**Affirmation 4, F.L.O.W.: "I look for the positive messages of light in every challenging situation."**
෴

This affirmation is definitely easier said than done. If the Universe had not showered me with brilliant puzzle pieces that came together and pulled me out of yucky situations, then I would not be saying these words with confidence. In case you missed my saying this earlier, my new favorite four-letter word that begins with the letter "F" is "flow." It used to be that other F-word, but today I see things differently. When my internal systems flow smoothly, I enjoy astounding mental clarity and robust emotional and physical comfort. Few things can "ruffle my feathers" these days. What used to rock my boat now rolls off my back (quack, quack). *F.L.O.W.* —*Feel Light Offering Wisdom* is a great acronym for how I envision living in my body during my stay on this planet. Although I was born into an environment of fear and anxiety over being different *from* other people and different *than* what was expected of me, I eventually chose the path of honoring exactly who I am. These days, I easily move my body without the weight of self-imposed expectations shaped by family heritage and society. With my butt off the pity-pot, I can take action without much subconscious resistance, thus saving me much time and energy! I have found that if you think or say to yourself "I will be in pain (be poor, lonely, or sick) for the rest of my life," you will likely create this reality for yourself and possibly your descendants. However, if you do the opposite, you can use that same power to release what weighs you down. Life is so much easier when we choose thoughts that shine like vibrant sunlight and share our "a-ha" moments and laughter with others.

With this healing-and-growth mindset you, too, can transform failures into successes to gain victory. A Self-Care Vigilante steps back from the pile of vomit and takes a deep breath to reconnect with the Universe of infinite options. Rather than shoving our feet into others' shoes and trying to make them fit, we build a shoe around each foot and move forward with comfort, dignity, and *F.L.O.W.* ⚘

**Affirmation 5, Give Permission: "I give myself permission to be human and embrace my imperfect ways."** ◌

This affirmation is a fun one for me. I is human. Me makes misteaks. This is coming from a formerly anal-retentive perfectionist who thought even the word "perfect" was not good enough for the meaning it conveyed. As a child, I drew perfect lines to make perfect columns down each page of my IZOD notebook. I used this ledger to grade myself each day. If my books or my coat slipped onto the floor as I crossed the living room after school, I earned a minus in my notebook. If my hair was out of place or my shirt was crooked when I caught my reflection in a window or mirror, I earned another minus. No wonder I closed my eyes while drinking from a whiskey bottle!

Whenever I aim to do something perfectly, the joke is on me. Thank goodness for my new habit of pausing and checking myself to stop the insanity. It took me years to truly understand the unfortunate impact of my perfectionism on other people. I deprived them of seeing my true self by hiding behind my duties at home or at work. Life on this planet is not about being a creature that performs perfectly. For my mental and physical health, permission to flop would be a success.

Long before I was even born, multiple generations exhibited compulsive perfectionism. Grateful for energy-based tools that support deeper levels of healing, I dropped the heavy baggage inherited from my ancestors to make my hands available for creating beauty. Thank you for the good genes, Grandma, but this crazy cycle stops here! Prayers to you in the celestial realm and to all those that came before me.

**Affirmation 6, Invite Power: "I invite a power that is greater than myself to heal me inside and out." ○%**

If I were a brain surgeon, I would have operated on myself. That was the old me. For my sake and yours, it is a good thing that I do not take credit for being able to control the sun, moon, planets, oceans, people, places, or things. The sun rises and sets because of a power greater than myself. What a terrific idea! I am neither omnipotent nor omniscient. If my behavior ever indicates otherwise, go ahead and pray for me. If you catch me trying to control what cannot be controlled, feel free to snap me out of it. I was not put here on Earth to drain myself. Time-debting is not part of the serenity equation. Just for today, *every day*, I invest in my soul.

The energy that heals my body cells, broken dreams, and misguided ego comes from a place within and beyond me. Being *one with the Universe* has its privileges, but anyone who chooses to align themselves continuously with this Source of limitless Power and Light can have all the peace and splendor that comes with unity. I trust where that power takes me while enjoying being the perfectly imperfect person that I am. As my spirit grows vibrant gardens (inside and out), yours can, too.

**Affirmation 7, Be Vibrant: "I release heavy energy and replace it with vibrant energy."** ❦

Many people have told me that I "glow." Rest assured, this has nothing to do with radiation exposure or anything of that sort. It is not because of my makeup, because I hardly wear any. I receive compliments while lounging in my baggy sweatshirts and jeans. It is possible that my Boston Red Sox gear has something to do with my looking so vibrant. (If that is the case, then you need not read any further; just wear the gear and you'll shine. Just kidding!)

In my experience, vibrancy comes from *within*. Through a person's eyes you can see a glow or flicker from the flame of the spirit. From one's voice, facial expression, or hand gestures, you can feel vibrations that grant you comfort when around that person. Through different ways we are able find satisfaction (mind), contentment (heart), serenity (spirit), and homeostasis (body). Striving for greater flow creates amazing glow.

I begin my day by trusting a Power that is greater than myself but also within me. Expanding my breath and energy field with this Power, I rise above any challenge that comes my way. Deliberately moving energy within my internal organs and systems, I promote the flow of blood, breath, nutrients, and waste. First thing in the morning, I flush out waste and make room for nutrients by drinking three glasses of warm-hot water. Then I greet and release trapped energy from my vital organs through tapping bi-laterally (two hands). After shaking loose what needs to leave my body, I spend one-on-one time with my Creator through prayer and meditation. ❦

Throughout the day, I continuously absorb fresh nutrients from food, sun, and laughter while releasing whatever my mind, body, and spirit no longer wish to carry. At the end of the day, I thank my Creator for everything and savor all my beautiful discoveries, accomplishments, and opportunities. Using tapping to dissolve any remaining regrets or heavy emotions, I then begin my night's journey into restorative sleep.

**Affirmation 8, Keep Intestines Happy: "I love, support, and grow all the good bacteria in my gut."** ❦

I am highly dedicated to keeping my small and large intestines happy in the effort to maintain a strong defense system against viruses, bacteria, food, and chemicals that weaken my body. At a deeper level, I want to hear very clearly what my gut intuition has to tell me. It is a truth meter that guides me to where and how I may be of maximum usefulness.

Every morning, I meditate while drinking my green juice filled with natural, energy-boosting minerals and vitamins. First, I bless the glass with a "Thank you," then take a sip of the juice with the thought, "I love," followed by another gulp, "support," next gulp, "and grow," deep breath and swallow with "all the good bacteria," and finally, "in my gut." I repeat this affirmation until all of the wonderful green juice is well on its way to empowering my immune system. How refreshing! ⚘

This short and simple process is my way of acknowledging the presence of healthy bacteria in my intestines and nourishing them. I actively encourage and cheer for the good guys to grow, multiply, and win over the bad guys. With this loving nudge, my team can achieve many victories throughout the day.

I move forward with confidence in my daily life, trusting that my intuition always will guide me toward goodness, safety, and light. People can see, hear, and feel this energy coming from me through my very expressive face, voice, and laughter. Even though I take wonderful steps forward, I leave it up to the Universe to respond. Witnessing fantastic results on a daily basis motivates me to keep my intestines happy and follow my gut intuition to the best of my ability.

**Affirmation 9, Embrace Oneness: "I embrace my connection to the Universe and everyone in it."** ⚘

Looking up at the stars at night, I connect the dots and see them glow, sparkle, and wink at me. In my body, too, are bright strings of holiday lights that connect all parts of me in magical ways. Imagining how energy flows through each atom of every cell of our bodies so greatly amazes me! We are all connected—past, present, and future —and bound together by human kindness and human atrocity. There are elements of both Heaven and Hell on Earth, but how frequently and sincerely we choose to expand the slices of Heaven, while learning from the slices of Hell, can make the difference between a fruitful life versus a downward spiral. I truly believe that recognizing beauty in our spirits can overpower any perception that we are broken or hopeless. Call me an optimist. ೮೪

Building the perception of a better world on Earth begins within each of us. I am less likely to disrupt anything filled with harmony, stability, and love when I practice self-compassion and self-care. Feeling serene and connected needs to begin with me. With a strong sense of purpose I create amazing tools for myself and for others. One day at a time, I do my part to ensure public safety by resting well, eating wisely, and surrounding myself with people who lift my spirits even higher. Together, we raise the level of vibrational frequency that spreads love and compassion throughout this planet by beginning within ourselves. Join us!

**Affirmation 10, Change Glasses: "I change my perspective or 'my glasses' whenever I feel stuck and willingly do things differently." ೮೪**

A Self-Care Vigilante embraces energy-boosting patterns of thought and behavior and stays off the human hamster wheel of insanity. The well-known definition of insanity is "repeating the same thing over and over, expecting different results." My sisters and brothers in Al-Anon (family support group for loved ones of alcoholics) know this all too well. My countless attempts to change people, places, and circumstances into my ways of thinking and doing often ended in frustration and exhaustion. I kept looking through the same lenses of my old glasses but was blind to the fact that everything was still blurry. *BLAH!* In addition to being stubborn, I allowed my undying loyalty to old familiar beliefs to lead me down dangerous paths, mentally and physically. Unaware of how distorted my perceptions were, I carried around a battlefield of internal conflict that kept me heavy and depressed—highly unstable ground for desired growth.

It takes time to peel the layers of an onion, as it does to take off the glasses that other people have worn, like those of my parents, teachers, friends, the media, government, corporations, and cultures. A Self-Care Vigilante welcomes opportunities to see things in a different light. When drawing conclusions and making decisions, I ask myself, "Through whose eyes am I seeing this person, situation, or problem?" Perhaps I have adopted *someone else's* belief systems about money, work, time, family, food, and relationships, but it has not served me in a healthy way. I now choose to use my tools and release that energy; my willingness to look through my *own* lenses and honor my unique perspectives will take me far. Yours will too.

Getting to the top of the Empire State Building requires effort, but the view is bright and splendid, challenging any remaining scarcity consciousness or tunnel vision. By stretching our mind's eye to see the bigger picture in every situation, we access infinite possibilities. With guidance from the Universe, we make wonderful decisions from a powerful place within each of us. Can it get any better than that? Absolutely!

**Affirmation 11, Welcome Water: "I thrive on growing, evolving, and changing continuously."**
ᘓ

This affirmation honors fluidity. Water is necessary for all life forms to grow, like people, animals, and forests on this planet. Every human being on Earth is comprised of over 70 percent water. Beyond needing water to survive, we partner with it and thrive through our connection.

One of water's properties is that it will go wherever it can. It is always moving and never at a complete standstill, even when it might appear to be. I welcome the movement of water and honor how it transforms my body. Witnessing the subtle power of energy at work greatly inspires me to pay close attention to all the shifts and changes within and around me. This fascination with movement of any form brings me great joy on this planet. Changes in physical space, time, internal flow, sound, rhythm, and more keep me growing and glowing. I stay "tuned in" to certain rhythms and vibrational frequencies that open doors for my true self to emerge brilliantly, thus leaving no room for distractions that hold me back.

If you have a moment of fearing change, think about water. Drink, touch, and flow like water. Expand the vibrant energy within your breath and stretch. Nourish everyone around you. Use your refreshed energy to create something you love. Acknowledge the fear and transform it with water and movement. See where this beautiful, natural process takes you! ᘓ

**Affirmation 12, Shine with Role Models:
"I surround myself with people who shine in their power, and I welcome their support."** ᘓ

During my early recovery in 12-step programs, a mentor shared with me, "Ilana, when you reach out your hand to greet someone, make sure that 50 percent of the time, you are putting out your hand to help pull someone up. The other 50 percent of the time, put out your hand to allow someone to pull *you* up." She was referring to my tendency to over-extend myself in helping people when I, too, was in need of nourishment. It was important to feed and to be fed in a balanced way. This message was vital to my long-term physical rehabilitation and recovery, as well as to other areas of my life.

Helping people brings me great joy, and it certainly reaffirms my own recovery. However,

I choose to reach out to mentors and role models who can spot my destructive patterns and lead me back to progress. I am willing to receive guidance from people who see their light and own their power, as wisdom from them helps me flow through my day with more grace, ease, and laughter. Watching my role models in action is so much fun, because they know their great value and continuously stretch themselves beyond their comfort zones to attain their visions. Witnessing their talents and accomplishments propels me to take action as well. There *are* many Self-Care Vigilantes like me—living on purpose and with passion. Join us and glow!

**Affirmation 13, Rise and Soar: "I gather the best tools from every personal development program and shape them for me."** ☙

There is plenty of time for me to do everything the Universe needs me to do. From mountains of knowledge and skills I might wish to acquire or develop, I choose carefully the teachers and programs that could help me achieve my goals. Many books, meetings, classes, workshops, events, and programs look delicious to me, as they promise success and happiness. My healing-and-growth mindset tells me that following my gut intuition is top priority and that there truly is a time and place for everything. I do not have to rush into anything, but at the same time, I must avoid resting on my laurels (which gets me nowhere). There is a healthy place somewhere in between the extremes; it behooves me to find it.

I have conversations with the Universe all the time, asking it to be obvious with answers as to what the next right thing to do is while making sure my motives are clean. At any time of the day or night, I pause and spot-check my impulsive tendencies, ego, or fears and ensure that they are not a factor in my decision-making. Doing diligence by making a "pros and cons" list can be an asset as well. However, my gut still leads the way.

Countless personal growth and development programs are available on the market. However, I choose to adopt the principles and tools that resonate most with me, let go of the ones that do not, and ask the Universe to lead me where I may serve and be served. When considering participation in programs, such as health, money, business, food, fitness, spirituality, and relationships, I embrace what honors my true self and ask, "Can I really blossom following this path or would I be designing a life to meet the approval of someone else?" My goal is to become the real me, spend time on Earth bringing my gifts and talents to fruition, and share these goodies with others. ✿

The happiest people I have met are the ones who invest energy into creating something inspired from within them. This is what makes us glad to get out of bed and step into our real shoes. No amount of money can buy this self-confidence that declares, "I dare to be me!" Living like someone I am not is exhausting, but granting myself permission to be vibrant creates a great legacy.

A Self-Care Vigilante always taps into the Universe for answers, inspiration, and strength. Remember to design the shoe around your foot so that you may carry your message to others from a stable, authentic place. Follow your gut intuition when you choose your mentors wisely; work with those who "walk their talk" and can help you achieve your goals with spiritual cleanliness. Like caterpillars in cocoons, Self-Care Vigilantes embrace the principles and tools that help us reach inward for inspiration so we may emerge as butterflies. ○3

**Affirmation 14, Lean Forward: "I lean forward to listen, learn, and engage." ○3**

I actively listen to people's words, watch their body language, and feel the vibration of their voices, while inviting harmony into our interactions. Paying attention to any part of my body that may experience sudden relaxation, relief, or joy, I engage more deeply with whatever ignites that goodness. When I feel sudden tension, heaviness, or pain anywhere, I thank my body for the warning signal, improve my posture, address any internal conflict (mental or emotional), and release waste to bring myself into a healthier space. Even though all kinds of information come my way every day, I continuously ask the Universe to point out what I must know versus what is none of my business.

A Self-Care Vigilante lives fully in the current moment and trusts that the Universe will present whatever is necessary when the time comes. Focusing on what is right in front of me, I lean forward and engage with others, especially mentors. Ongoing communication opens more doors to limitless options. Observing people while engaging with them, I learn both what to do and what not to do and cherish any reminder of that wisdom. I can pause at any moment to reassess top-priority goals and activities to achieve milestones and then cross finish lines with grace, ease, and laughter. ⁣☙

Each time we listen, learn, and engage with people on a consistent basis, we are forming new lines of energy exchange. Practicing the art of communication—actively connecting the dots (energy points) from one person to another—we live the principle of unity and build a conscious connection that becomes a power that is greater than the sum of its parts. United, we glow.

**Affirmation 15, Focus on Good: "I focus on all the good in my life and have confidence I can create more of it and flourish." ☙**

In my alpine ski training, I learned to pay close attention to the direction of my downhill shoulder. If my shoulder closest to the bottom of the mountain was pointing toward the trees, then that was where the rest of my body was headed. I certainly kissed a lot of trees—far too many to count. The same concept applies to goals and visions. When I focus on all the good I have in my life (over what I lack), then my goals and visions are more likely to come to fruition. On the other hand, by dwelling on all that I *do not* have, I am letting the good slip away and pushing away what I desire (Universal Law of Attraction and Repulsion). ○§

My long history of resistance, defiance, and rebellion kept me comfortable in misery, thanks to my focusing on everything that was missing in my life. I own my part in allowing more of the same: self-pity and scarcity. Sick and tired of being sick and tired, I had to find the slightest hint of willingness within me to break free from the multigenerational baggage of survivor's guilt I inherited from my family. The journey of overcoming guilt about living well and leaving struggles behind was tough but worth it. Letting go of old familiar ways was not a show of disrespect to the past but a commitment to shining a light for generations to come.

Personal experience has shown me that my human brain is extremely flexible and my nervous system can be retrained (neuroplasticity). Borrowing other people's optimism and belief in limitless possibilities, I rebuilt my immune system and overcame many deeper layers of self-destructive compulsions. In time, my own brew of optimism and enthusiasm gracefully emerged.

Tapping on the meridian points of my energy superhighway in my body was one of several powerful energy-based tools I used to reverse my subconscious resistance to the life I was meant to live. With guidance from highly skilled practitioners, many of my destructive patterns have dissipated. Closing the door on self-sabotage was heavenly. The process of releasing physical and emotional constipation created a tremendous amount of space for goodness to enter and nourish me. Today, vibrations of victory resonate throughout my body and in all areas of my life, as I celebrate my strengths, embrace my shadows, and allow the real me to rise up from the ashes and soar like the phoenix! ෬

**Affirmation 16, Live Authentically: "I show what I feel and embrace honesty and authenticity."** ෬

Many people have told me that my face is like an open book. This was after having spent decades hiding my thoughts and feelings behind a poker face that kept me safe during my childhood, as well as in the streets of New York and on all the jobs I have ever held. The life of former "mysterious me" was cool but exhausting. Perfectionism helped me to hide, and compulsive people-pleasing kept my illusion of inclusion alive. Although I received validation and awards for my work, I felt nothing. My lack of appreciation for myself left all the compliments and successes in the dust. My external world was incongruent with my inner life.

Today, I live the life of a Self-Care Vigilante in which nourishing my mind-body-soul connection with guidance from the Universe continues to outshine all else I have ever achieved. Each time

I unravel an internalized frown or fear, my face and posture wear a fresh new look that runs deep. My body releases extra weight from emotional burdens that no longer or never did serve me well, including thoughts, feelings, actions, and consequences I felt obligated to carry, but which actually belonged to other people. A daily regimen of self-care activities progressively dissolves any heavy energy from my past and present trauma and those of my loved ones.

*Being authentic, fully transparent, and walking my talk is a fabulous way to exist on this planet.* My old fears and subconscious resistance to change no longer hold me back. Instead, I live courageously and on purpose without apology. The real me thrives! 03

**Affirmation 17, Embrace Time: "I connect ideas, energy, and solutions wherever I go." 03**

This affirmation honors my profound awareness of the abundance of time. Time is one—past, present, and future. What was, is now, and what will be is all connected. I do believe that whenever we are ready, we can travel through time to find solutions. This may sound as if I have "gone quantum," bonkers, or both. But it works for me. Entertaining the idea that we live in the curved space of time, I say "Why not?" After all, we live on the curved surface of this planet, although some people might still need to hold onto the idea that the earth is flat.

I used to panic a lot, struck by fear of losing time, missing out on something, falling behind, and feeling excluded. There was not enough time to do everything, and I was always late. From childhood, my night-owl brain never completely woke up until lunchtime. Having to catch up from being behind everyone else started at the very beginning of my visit on Earth.

Today, I have an amazing relationship with time. A Self-Care Vigilante, I love fully living in the moment and staying in alignment with what the Universe reveals as true priorities. The more I meditate and connect with the Universe, the greater my serenity and the sense of being cared for, carried, and fully supported in every way. Throughout the day I ask the simple question, "Where does the Universe need me right now?" This activates my intuition to engage and follow Divine guidance. Answers pop into my mind, natural vibrant energy lifts me to rise to the occasion, and many "just right" solutions move into place. I live each day connecting ideas, energy, and solutions with tons of heartfelt laughter. You can, too. Embrace the beauty, curvature, and wisdom of time. ☙

**Affirmation 18, Give a Voice: "I tap into my subconscious mind and give it the voice it deserves to have." ☙**

My body, spirit, and mind are often in agreement and alignment, because they now work together as a team, rather than vying for domination and battling back and forth. After decades of trying to be the boss, my mind still enjoys being very much needed and relevant but is able to let go of controlling and performing functions it was never designed to do in the first place. Listening to guidance from my body and spirit leads to wonderful outcomes my mind could never have imagined. Life is so exciting!

Every day, my entire team—body, spirit, and mind—reaches for things to celebrate while they work collaboratively. Whenever each part is called to rise to the occasion, the others trust the leader and take a step back but are ready to engage if needed to serve as a resource. This grants me vibrant energy to bring enthusiasm into everything I do, including getting delicious, high-quality sleep, absorbing great nutrients from food and people, tapping out negative thoughts, and waving "Farewell" to my beautiful poop. Hallelujah!

**Affirmation 19, Acknowledge Polarity:**
**"I embrace dark and light sides <u>within</u> me and allow both to work <u>for</u> me."** ∞

While acknowledging my fears and shortcomings, I celebrate goodness in my heart and a long list of positive attributes. Embracing my shadows and failures, I allow them to help me feel whole, complete, and loved. Real self-confidence to move forward in life comes from feeling happy about being perfectly imperfect—which really means that I am just fine the way I am, for now, but am ready to discover more of my good stuff. Making adjustments here and there toward how I would like to be or what I would like to do is far more powerful than sitting in shame, guilt, or remorse. These days, fears and failures still come but pass quickly. Heavy, dark moments are short and infrequent. I embrace all of it to create new forms of joy.

Where there is darkness, there is light. I acknowledge but detach from all the skewed and distorted perceptions of myself. Freedom from seeing myself as a victim is priceless. When people invite me to their pity parties, I thank them but decline, for the old dangerous neighborhoods in my mind are now beautiful fields where I play, create, and laugh. My healing-and-growth mindset guides me to see that I truly have more options than I think, no matter how bad things look or feel at the moment. What a tremendous blessing!

**Affirmation 20, Dissolve Judgment: "I dissolve sarcastic and judgmental thoughts instantaneously."** ❧

A smirk came across my face when a psychotherapist presented the idea that my sarcastic comments revealed I was feeling threatened by something. Highly defensive and angry, I tossed out that idea, instantaneously. Sarcasm was a great way to showcase my sense of humor. My being a sharp shooter was just fine, as I was born with the right to be critical. Eventually, after witnessing other people's biting words of sarcastic disapproval toward themselves and others, I began to feel the rawness in the vibration of underlying anger inside them. What I then realized was that sarcasm, judgment, fear, and anger were all connected. What those people had—insecurity—I did not want. What they did not have—self-confidence—was what I desired. ❧

Consistently removing non-productive, non-loving garbage from my thoughts, words, and actions is definitely worth the effort. My days flow smoothly when I quickly dissolve any sarcastic and judgmental thoughts, resentments, jealousy, arrogance, self-righteousness, indignation, fear, and self-battery. I continuously release unnecessary weight from my body, allowing sacks of burden to melt from my shoulders, heart, and waistline. Freedom from emotional constipation has given me real confidence to step up to the plate and face what the Universe presents me. With moaning and groaning behind me, I have emerged, glowing with every bite-sized step, to improve the quality of my life and of those around me and beyond. No more wild and crazy chaos. Delicious *freedom from self-righteous anger* found here.

**Affirmation 21, Seek Mission: "I accept my presence and mission on this planet." ❧**

The Universe did not grant my request when I asked for a small log cabin in the mountains without another human being around for miles. Something in me knew that my cabin was not coming anytime soon, and I eventually let go of my dream of living in complete isolation. I learned that the Universe was not ignoring my wishes but helping me fulfill my mission on this planet. Little by little, it revealed that what brings me true joy has nothing to do with isolating myself and disregarding the world. Quite the contrary: my passion is to use my voice to help soothe people and animals, bringing them comfort and laughter!

It was a dark time in late 2011 when my vocal cords locked up and I could barely utter a sound. Even though I found people and situations funny, I could not laugh. My face lit up and mouth opened, but not a "ha" or "ho" came out. CRPS confused my digestive system, and non-narcotic pain medications upset my stomach. Acid went up my esophagus, eroded the tissue lining, and spilled into my larynx. Everything was inflamed, swollen, and on fire. This was a form of isolation I had not bargained for and could not escape.

"If I ever get my real voice back," I negotiated with the Universe, while staring at the stars and planets, "I promise never to take it for granted again. I will use it to deliver whatever you want me to share with the world." Regaining my real voice required months and months of hard work and discipline. After seeing many specialists and nutritionists, trying a dozen medications, and making many food, exercise, and lifestyle changes, here I am: able to hear my original voice and, with great awe, experience the vibration it produces and sends throughout my body. Being imprisoned in my own body has set me free. I am now able to share my voice with you through audiobooks and other deeply meaningful ways. Reconciling with my body and living on purpose has been so very rewarding! ⚘

**Affirmation 22, Celebrate Inner Light: "I see my light and celebrate its power to bring relief to others."** ⚘

I like the expression, "If you spot it, you've got it." The Universal Law of Oneness explains that we are all connected. The Law of Emergence reveals that the goodness we begin to see in ourselves and in others has been within us all along. Twelve-step recovery literature reminds us that when we dislike something about another person, it is time to put the focus back on cleaning up our "insides" to make the world a better place. Each and every one of us serves as a mirror for one another.

Using the transitive axiom of geometry, which stated, "If A=B and B=C, then A=C," I realized that there must have been some goodness and light in me, since I was able to see much beauty in others. Focusing on our character assets, in addition to our shortcomings, is especially critical to all stages and types of recovery; my foot can attest to that. Seeing ourselves through distorted lenses can magnify our negative qualities and set us up for relapsing into old behavior.

Balance is key. Deliberate recovery means that we embrace good and bad, leave judgment behind, and move forward in creating new habits, healthy bodies, loving relationships, astounding artwork, and robust businesses. Let us actively celebrate our light and trust that we are truly worthy! ℭℨ

**Affirmation 23: Find Serious Humor: "I find humor in my past and in my non-traditional ways."** ℭℨ

When I first began performing comedy, my intention was to be surrounded by funny people, letting others entertain and distract me from my pain and misery. However, people soon found my presence enjoyable. My personal drama and trauma began to make people laugh while crying and cry while laughing. There I was, on stage, with a walker on bad pain nights and two canes on better nights. Performing stand-up/sit-down comedy was a great emotional outlet for me. Occasionally, I confessed to audiences that they were there for my benefit when I was unable to find my shrink or therapist. Free counseling with no co-pay—woohoo!

Learning self-acceptance through stage work has been an unexpected yet incredible blessing. I rarely talk in depth about my injuries and illnesses on stage; taking breaks from focusing on my physical limitations is very healthy. However, I love sharing about my adventures as a "confused person with clarity." My first name is Greek, and my last name is Bulgarian, but I am genetically Chinese with a Korean maiden name and the heart of a Puerto Rican. Always having thought of myself as a guy in a chick's body, I occasionally perform stand-up/sit-down comedy as a drag queen (a man, dressed as a diva, who performs on stage with full female persona) to further explore my feminine side. A recovered alcoholic, I still think I drove better under the influence of whiskey, for I am neurologically different from everyone else (and not because I'm Chinese).

As an act of service to my country, I occasion-ally warn audiences not to go to the bathroom while I am on stage because of my abandonment issues. If that is not intimacy, then I do not know what is. A person in my shoes could take this one step further by saying that since I am a guy in a chick's body, then my being married to a man means that I must be gay. However, I find women very attractive, as well, and so, I am also a straight male. That clarifies everything.

The point of this story is that beautiful experiences can come to us when we allow our inner conflicts, shortcomings, and shadows to meet the sunlight of the Spirit. The Universe continuously lines up all the elements—even from unlikely places—to bless us with joy and laughter!

**Affirmation 24, Protect Inner Flame: "I detach from whatever dims my inner flame."** ⟡

When I close my eyes, I can see a dancing white flame, playfully flickering on a candle sitting high in the middle of a roomy cave. This space is where my soul rests. My job is to protect this flame while making sure that nothing restricts its freedom to move in any direction it likes. Oxygen feeds my flame. If I sense that it is struggling, removing whatever prevents it from dancing freely is my priority. I secure the happiness of my soul.

My job is to protect my inner flame by detaching from whatever chokes its oxygen supply. Because I am the one who creates or invites limitations that block my flame from freedom and, at the same time, the one who can dissolve those limitations, I must grant myself permission to stretch deeply into creativity in order to save my spirit. Developing new goals and welcoming healthy role models into my life to journey with me is empowering. Living my mission on this planet is juicy and filled with delightful surprises; anything less would feel empty and bleak.

I detach myself from stagnation and paralysis to honor my commitment to vibrancy and self-compassion. It is my responsibility, as a Self-Care vigilante, to cultivate an environment that continuously protects and replenishes my dancing inner flame. We bless ourselves when we cut the threads that tie us to unrest, mistrust, and chaos. Treasuring our inner flame magically lifts others around us and fuels a spiritual power plant that generates harmony for all.

**Affirmation 25, Forgive: "I forgive myself and everyone who is unavailable or unable to help me grow stronger and upward."** ଔ

The bad news first: whenever I think someone owes me an apology, the resentment burdens my body with heavy energy, decreases my productivity, and blocks me from experiencing great joy. The good news is that letting go of grudges and animosity liberates me from constipation—physical, mental, emotional, and spiritual. I admit that holding a grudge may feel like the right thing to do for a while, but converting poop to fertilizer grows gardens. Poop that sits without transformation is nothing more than a pile of sheep doo. No offense, my fellow sheep!

I feel lighter and more hopeful than ever before because of my commitment to keeping the resentment-making machine between my ears turned off. The drama queen within me, also known to be a queen of self-abandonment, denial, and so on, has laid her crown to rest. Now wearing a grass skirt, she bathes in sunshine upon white sandy beaches and crystal-clear blue waters.

You, too, can free yourself by putting down your judge's gavel, taking off the robe, and deliberately pursuing a life without handcuffs, blindfolds, and heavy suitcases that no longer serve you. Save your body, mind, and spirit by reaching out to people who glow with confidence, compassion, and creativity. Be a Self-Care Vigilante and allow these role models to show you how to face each day with the Source of unlimited possibilities that never stops conspiring to love and support you.

**Affirmation 26, Serve with a Full Cup: "I give to others when my cup is full, because I am a Self-Care Vigilante!"** ☞

I listen carefully to guidance from the Universe when offering emotional support, vibrant energy, and spiritual insight. Practicing self-compassion is one of the most honorable ways to be of service. Maintaining healthy boundaries is a very precious component of spiritual growth and expansion. I find space and time to absorb nourishment for all parts of me—mind, body, and spirit—to be ready for anything the Universe deems as a priority for me.

**As Chief Executive Officer (CEO) of my body, I pause throughout the day to eat life-reaffirming foods and drink clean water, release unnecessary thoughts, fears, or heavy energy, and shape time to take deep breaths and reconnect with the Universe.** My belief is that talking to ourselves in kind, gentle, and nurturing ways—the opposite of self-battery— contributes to delivering and sustaining higher vibrational frequencies to all life forms on our planet. Using warm-to-hot water to restore, cleanse, and revitalize our internal systems is extremely effective in reducing the impact of environmental contaminants and increasing our vitality.

These and other self-care practices bring us to a place where we can be truly honest within ourselves and in agreement among mind, body, and spirit with other people. Honesty is a spiritual principle upon which everything else is built. Combining honesty with self-care practices cultivates serenity and intuitive insight. Let us walk our talk with integrity and share our well-nourished inner gardens with the world! ❧

## From Groaning to Glowing

Many people expressed their pity for me because of the loss of my ability to participate in life the way I used to before my health fell apart. "Such a young woman should not have to use a walker, give up her career, and struggle with so little money," they said. Thank you, but no thank you. I have given that negative energy to the earth beneath my feet and asked Mother Nature to recycle and transform it into beautiful energy that grows real and metaphorical gardens.

My symptoms have reminded me to stay focused on taking deep breaths through the pain, to search for doctors who are willing to guide me, and to pick up the phone to ask for help to do the many things I am no longer able to do for myself. Layer by layer, I have learned how to live life without depending on alcohol, nicotine, and caffeine; taking narcotic pain meds; eating wheat and most types of sugars and dairy products; relying upon credit cards; masturbating over fantasies; and envying people for doing things I cannot. In place of those activities, I celebrate life—drink water (with cucumber), eat raw veggies (the crunchier the better), invite spiritually clean streams of income, spend carefully, blossom beautifully in a monogamous relationship, and enjoy my connection with the Universe and everything in it—whether or not I agree with what is happening around me.

Each day, my body still requires at least four hours of special attention and care for me to function at a moderate level. At least I am able to reach for things that drop or spill onto the floor, drive my car without the left-foot accelerator pedal I needed for years, and step in and out of the shower without risking a fall. Throughout the day, I massage my internal organs by taking deep breaths, stretching different parts of my body, and using Chi Gong and tapping to release tightness and pain. Frequently, I ask my body what it needs, listen for priorities from the Universe, rearrange my activities in alignment with those priorities, and lie down to rest my legs on pillows before and after each activity.

On good days, I go to the gym, serve others, ride my bike in a park, and grocery shop without assistance. Occasionally, I country line-dance, travel on airplanes, participate in speaking engagements, and perform comedy on stage. Someday soon, I will be able to put my feet in ski boots and enjoy the bunny slopes—a far cry from black diamond moguls, but I am learning to be all right with that. ❧

From groaning to glowing, I have found ways to feel reenergized, inside and out. Today, I truly *F.L.O.W.* Feeling light while basking in the Light of the Universe, I allow all collaborating parts of me to offer people wisdom, hope, and laughter. Had I continued swimming in a pool of self-pity and victim energy, my story would have ended in hopelessness. Instead, my Self-Care Vigilante healing-and-growth mindset inspired me to commit to attaining higher levels of creativity beyond my imagination.

My daily practice of inviting inspirational thoughts that ignite action toward developing, protecting, and growing a mind-body-spirit connection with the Universe has skyrocketed my success rate in crossing countless finish lines in all areas of my life. This self-care regimen has 1) delivered tremendous laughter, the best medicine for healing and preventing illness or injury, 2) guided me in wisely investing time and money in myself, not only for me but also for public health and safety, and 3) helped me in creating a platform to serve the world from a truly authentic space.

**I continue to practice what I preach and offer hope that inner peace is possible under any condition; connecting with the vast Universe ignites our creative energy and gives us limitless reasons to celebrate on Earth.** Can it get any better than that? Absolutely! Daring to dream beyond the power of my mind alone, I allow my guardian angels to carry me to new destinations, as I enjoy each delicious point along the way.

Join me in my journey. Let us tap into the Universe for recovery, discovery, and flight! ❧

ॐ

Deliberate recovery is consciously following our gut intuition and taking bite-sized steps to invite life-affirming nutrients into the body, mind, and spirit simultaneously. This attitude-in-action allows our natural talents and gifts to emerge as we accept courage, wisdom, and strength that arrive through our spiritual umbilical cord to the Universe.

## Foundation Statement

As every living and non-living entity in the Universe is connected energetically, we must promote the flow of energy at the cellular level of our being to live in harmony within ourselves and with others. Together, we can vibrate and glow in unison as a beacon of indescribable hope and love on this planet.

## Exercise for Chapter Nine

*Ilana's Guided Meditation for GLIDING ACROSS the FINISH LINE*

"I choose to pace myself gently, like a marathon runner, so that I may GLIDE across the finish line in all areas of my life with GRACE, EASE, and LAUGHTER."
ᘓ　—Ilana Kristeva

In this guided meditation exercise, you will enjoy taking beautiful, deep breaths in between powerful images of your vision to accomplish goals with dignity and self-respect. Since creating this personal mantra years ago, I have been saying it out loud during my walks, workouts, or quiet time each day. It is a wonderful experience to hear, see, and feel that I am reclaiming my life, one breath at a time. May you be re-energized with hope and motivation as you glide across many finish lines every single day!

Below is guidance for your meditation. Begin by speaking each word as clearly as possible, either out loud or in your head. Whenever you see breath marks (ᘓ), take a deep breath IN through your NOSE, hold the breath for one to two seconds, and then, gently let the breath OUT through your LIPS.

Inhale deeply and say, "I" ᘓ

Inhale deeply and say, "I choose" ᘓ

Inhale deeply and say, "I choose to" ᘓ

Inhale... "I choose to **pace**" ○წ

Inhale... "I choose to pace **myself**" ○წ

Inhale... "I choose to pace myself **gently**" ○წ

Inhale... "I choose to pace myself gently [inhale] **like**" ○წ

Inhale... "I choose to pace myself gently [inhale] like **a**" ○წ

Inhale... "I choose to pace myself gently [inhale] like a **marathon**" ○წ

Inhale... "I choose to pace myself gently [inhale] like a marathon **runner**" ○წ

Inhale... "I choose to pace myself gently [inhale] like a marathon runner [inhale] **so**" ○წ

Inhale... "I choose to pace myself gently [inhale] like a marathon runner [inhale] so **that**" ○წ

Inhale... "I choose to pace myself gently [inhale] like a marathon runner [inhale] so that **I**" ○წ

Inhale... "I choose to pace myself gently [inhale] like a marathon runner [inhale] so that I **may**" ○წ

Inhale... "I choose to pace myself gently [inhale] like a marathon runner [inhale] so that I may **GLIDE**" ○წ

Inhale... "I choose to pace myself gently [inhale] like a marathon runner [inhale] so that I may GLIDE [inhale] **across**" ○წ

Inhale... "I choose to pace myself gently [inhale] like a marathon runner [inhale] so that I may GLIDE [inhale] across **the**" ଔ

Inhale... "I choose to pace myself gently [inhale] like a marathon runner [inhale] so that I may GLIDE [inhale] across the **FINISH**" ଔ

Inhale... "I choose to pace myself gently [inhale] like a marathon runner [inhale] so that I may GLIDE [inhale] across the FINISH **LINE**" ଔ

Inhale... "I choose to pace myself gently [inhale] like a marathon runner [inhale] so that I may GLIDE [inhale] across the FINISH LINE [inhale] **in**" ଔ

Inhale... "I choose to pace myself gently [inhale] like a marathon runner [inhale] so that I may GLIDE [inhale] across the FINISH LINE [inhale] in **all**" ଔ

Inhale... "I choose to pace myself gently [inhale] like a marathon runner [inhale] so that I may GLIDE [inhale] across the FINISH LINE [inhale] in all **areas**" ଔ

Inhale... "I choose to pace myself gently [inhale] like a marathon runner [inhale] so that I may GLIDE [inhale] across the FINISH LINE [inhale] in all areas **of**" ଔ

Inhale... "I choose to pace myself gently [inhale] like a marathon runner [inhale] so that I may GLIDE [inhale] across the FINISH LINE [inhale] in all areas of **my**" ଔ

Inhale... "I choose to pace myself gently [inhale]

like a marathon runner [inhale] so that I may GLIDE [inhale] across the FINISH LINE [inhale] in all areas of my **life**" ○弓

Inhale... "I choose to pace myself gently [inhale] like a marathon runner [inhale] so that I may GLIDE [inhale] across the FINISH LINE [inhale] in all areas of my life [inhale] **with**" ○弓

"I choose to pace myself gently [inhale] like a marathon runner [inhale] so that I may GLIDE [inhale] across the FINISH LINE [inhale] in all areas of my life [inhale] with **GRACE**" ○弓

Inhale... "I choose to pace myself gently [inhale] like a marathon runner [inhale] so that I may GLIDE [inhale] across the FINISH LINE [inhale] in all areas of my life [inhale] with GRACE, **EASE**" ○弓

Inhale... "I choose to pace myself gently [inhale] like a marathon runner [inhale] so that I may GLIDE [inhale] across the FINISH LINE [inhale] in all areas of my life [inhale] with GRACE, EASE, **and**" ○弓

Inhale... "I choose to pace myself gently [inhale] like a marathon runner [inhale] so that I may GLIDE [inhale] across the FINISH LINE [inhale] in all areas of my life [inhale] with GRACE, EASE, and **LAUGHTER!**"
○弓

"Yes, ○弓 I choose to pace myself gently ○弓 like a marathon runner, ○弓 so that I may GLIDE ○弓 across the FINISH LINE ○弓 in all areas of my life ○弓 with GRACE, ○弓 EASE, ○弓 and **LAUGHTER!**" ○弓

# Appendices

# APPENDIX A:

## Tapping Meridian Points

Throughout each of our bodies, we have a vast meridian system that I like to refer to as our *energy superhighway*. Flowing through our highways is the energy (electricity) we need to keep all our internal organs and systems functioning at their best. Some highways come close to the surface of our skin and offer us almost direct access to them. These access points are known as *meridian points,* so that we can touch and connect with the insides of our bodies without surgery. Chiropractors, acupuncturists, and tapping practitioners actively use their knowledge of the connection between the surface of the skin and internal body parts (cutaneo-visceral reflex) to help increase positive flow of energy, improve blood circulation, stimulate production of new cells, and restore our bodies back to health. ☙

The following are tapping meridian points used in Progressive Energy Field Tapping (or Pro EFT™)—based on Emotional Freedom Technique (EFT)—to support the release of stuck energy and improve the overall energy flow throughout our bodies.* In most situations, we use our left hand to tap the left side of side of our body and our right hand on the right side of our body at the same time (bilateral tapping). This moves energy on both right and left sides simultaneously to promote greater balance, harmony, and healing. At the top of our head, we need only one hand to reach the center-rear tapping point (crown or CR).

Before starting, however, we drink water to rehydrate and support the flow of energy that may be trapped, stuck, or going in the wrong direction. After tapping we drink even more water to flush out waste and electromagnetic particles that do not belong in our bodies, similar to rinsing dishes after scrubbing the dirt or rinsing the soap off our bodies when we shower or bathe. ∞

KC:   Karate Chop Point (Small Intestine Meridian). This is the starting point for all tapping sequences, especially while focusing on "Reversals" in the Mindfulness Medita-tion and Tapping Exercises at the end of each chapter in this book.

EB:   Between the Eyebrows (Urinary Bladder Meridian)

SE:   Sides of the Eyes (Gall Bladder Meridian)

UE:   Under the Eyes (Stomach Meridian)

UN:   Under the Nose (Governing Vessel)

CH:   Chin (Central Vessel)

CB:   Start of Collar Bone (Kidney Meridian)

UA:   Under the Arms (Spleen Meridian)

LV:   Front Ribs, Below the Nipples (Liver Meridian)

WR:   Wrists (where Lung, Heart/Pericardium and Large Intestine Meridians come together, from fingers to wrists)

CR:   Crown or Top of Head (Governing Vessel) ∞

## PROFESSIONAL INSTRUCTION
## AND GUIDANCE

Please take personal responsibility in seeking guidance from an EFT or Pro EFT practitioner who can accompany you in rising to new levels of self-discovery in a safe and healthy environment. There is no guarantee that EFT and Pro EFT will produce the same outcomes for you as for other people. However, professionals can demonstrate how to use Reversals most effectively in the Mindfulness Meditation and Tapping Exercises, as well as any additional sequence rounds for clearing away heavy energy and re-igniting vibrancy within and around you. ☙

*\*The Foundation Statement for Progressive Energy Field Tapping (Pro EFT™), developed by EFT Master Lindsay Kenny, is the Discovery Statement for EFT: "The cause of all negative emotions is a disruption in the body's energy system." — Gary Craig, founder of Emotional Freedom Technique (EFT), based on the work of the late Dr. Roger Callahan, founder of Thought Field Therapy (TFT).*

# APPENDIX B:

## Expanded Version of Chapter One Exercise:

*Ilana's Mindfulness Meditation and Tapping Exercise for EMOTIONAL BODY COMFORT in a 5-part Format (adapted Progressive Energy Field Tapping, or Pro EFT\*)*

The following tapping exercise presents an idea of how to use EFT and Pro EFT tools for neutralizing and releasing stuck energy and negative emotions for greater health and well-being. Although there are technical procedures involved in this exercise, the art of tapping requires the use of gut intuition to read how the body's energetic system responds to both the physical tapping on the meridian points and the words that instinctively emerge during the process. Please refer to *APPENDIX A: Tapping Meridian Points* and say the words aloud while relaxing and tapping. ∞

The bulleted Reversals are adaptations of a powerful Pro EFT™ process of *Reversal Neutralization.* Saying Reversals while you tap on the KC points (both hands, if possible) helps to neutralize any energy in your body that may be scrambled or flowing in the wrong direction. Please note that calming down scrambled or reversed energy is not the entire tapping process for resolving issues—physical, emotional, or financial. For full application of these statements, please seek guidance from an EFT or Pro EFT practitioner or from a psychotherapist who uses tapping.** Select someone whom you feel can support you in rising to new levels of self-discovery.

REMEMBER: Please drink some water before, during, and after this exercise. This is a vital part of cleansing and refreshing your body.

Please take a DEEP breath and scan your body from head to toe. Describe where you feel any tightness, pressure, pain, or other types of discomfort. Identify some of the strongest emotions you are feeling right now. Rate the intensity of the most uncomfortable area or most intense emotion with a SUDS (Subjective Units of Distress) reading on a scale of zero to ten (ten=most intense physical or emotional distress and zero=absolutely no physical pain, discomfort, or emotional distress). Write down your number on a piece of paper before tapping.

❖ Reversal 1: KC: "Even though my frustration and disappointment in my body's lack of cooperation is keeping me from getting pain relief and good sleep, there's a part of me that is *not* ready to let it go, for whatever reason. (Maybe I'm an unlucky person, I'm being punished, or I did this to myself and deserve it.)*** But I want to love, accept, and respect myself anyway." ☙

*Note: Slowly repeat the above Reversal <u>three times</u> before moving forward with two or three rounds of the venting sequence, such as:*

EB: "This frustration"
SE: "This pain"
UE: "This disappointment"
UN: "Is keeping me stuck"
CH: "I don't feel safe"
CB: "I can't get relief"
UA: "Nothing seems to work"
LV: "My body doesn't want to cooperate"
WR: "It won't let go of my misery"
CR: "I don't know why"
EB: "Oh yes, I do"
SE: "No, I don't"
UE: "Maybe I have an idea"
UN: "Maybe I don't"
CH: "But my body knows why"
CB: "Maybe it's telling me ___"
UA: "But a part of me won't let that go"
LV: "For whatever reason ___"
WR: "But I want to honor that part of me anyway"
CR: "I want to love, accept, and respect myself"
ෆ

Take a DEEP breath, drink water, and relax. Follow these rounds with a SUDS (Subjective Units of Distress) reading to measure degree of relief (for example, 10 or 9 drops to 8 or 7) prior to the next Reversal.

❖ Reversal 2: KC: "Even though my agitation and anxiety about my condition and pain is blocking me from truly relaxing and healing in peace, I honor the part of me that's not letting it go and thank my body for telling me it needs my help. And I love, accept, and respect myself." ☪

*Note: Slowly repeat the above Reversal once or twice before moving forward with the sequence, such as:*

EB:     "This feeling of _____"
SE:     "It's blocking me from relief "
UE:     "And affecting my ability to _____"
UN:     "I've been dealing with this for too long"
CH:     "I'm tired of feeling _____"
CB:     "I tried to get rid of it by _____"
UA:     "It worked for other people"
LV:     "Why doesn't it work for me?"
WR:     "This is nuts"
CR:     "I don't deserve this pain"
EB:     "I don't know why I am so stuck"
SE:     "Maybe I deserve it"
UE:     "Maybe I don't"
UN:     "Maybe this discomfort reminds me of another situation"
CH:     "When I was extremely agitated and anxious about _____"
CB:     "Maybe these situations are connected"
UA:     "Or maybe they're not"
LV:     "Even though I'm not sure"
WR:     "My body cells might remember"

CR:     "Thank you body for getting my attention"
UA:     "And even though I'm feeling _____"
LV:     "I'm willing to help my body begin to let it go because _____"
WR:     "And I love, accept, and respect myself"
CR:     "Starting now, no matter what" ❧

Take a DEEP breath, drink water, and relax. Follow these rounds with a SUDS (Subjective Units of Distress) reading to measure some degree of relief (for example, 8 or 7 drops to 5 or 4) prior to the next Reversal.

❖     Reversal 3: KC: "Even though this pain, anxiety, and fatigue in my body is still holding me back from moving forward in different areas of my life, I thank my body for carrying me this far and ask it to forgive my impatience. I love and accept myself and offer the tender love and care I need and deserve." ❧

Note: Slowly repeat the above Reversal once or twice before moving forward with the sequence, such as:

EB:     "This remaining pain in my _____"
SE:     "All my insecurities about _____"
UE:     "I can't seem to move forward"
UN:     "I'm tired of not making much progress"
CH:     "I'm tired of feeling stuck"
CB:     "This has affected my _____"
UA:     "I've been suffering far too long"
LV:     "But I need to release this anger"

| WR: | "I want to release this grief" |
|---|---|
| CR: | "I have to get over this pain" |
| EB: | "Thank you, body, for letting me start here" |
| SE: | "And for carrying me this far" |
| UE: | "Despite everything I've done to ignore you" |
| UN: | "Or neglect you" |
| CH: | "Or keep you quiet" |
| CB: | "For whatever reason" |
| UA: | "Please forgive me for being impatient with you" |
| LV: | "That didn't work too well did it?" |
| WR: | "But I'm willing to hear you now" |
| CR: | "I may not know how to help you" |
| EB: | "But I do know one thing" |
| SE: | "I want us to work together" |
| UE: | "I'll make you my partner" |
| UN: | "Because I deeply and completely love and accept myself" |
| UH: | "And I'll offer you compassion, body" |
| CB: | "Compassion will help me heal" |
| UA: | "Heal and move forward" |
| LV: | "Whether or not I think I deserve it" |
| WR: | "Whether or not I think I can get better" |
| CR: | "Because I love and accept myself deeply and completely" ෲ |

Take a DEEP breath, drink water, and relax. Follow these rounds with a SUDS (Subjective Units of Distress) reading to measure degree of relief (for example, 5 or 4 drops to 3 or 2). Continue with additional rounds if SUDS is higher than zero or one.

If SUDS is one but unable to drop down to zero, then use a very powerful EFT technique called the *9-Point Gamut* to bring SUDS down to absolute zero. (Please learn about this technique from basic EFT resources.) Then move forward with the next Reversal.

❖ Reversal 4: KC: "Even though this remaining discomfort in my body, mind, and heart has held me back from saying 'Yes' to wonderful opportunities in my life, I *choose* to let go of my stress, anger, and fear and find courage, hope, and laughter. I embrace my "insides" and "outsides," because I love and accept myself deeply and completely." ❧

*Note: Slowly repeat the above Reversal once or twice before moving forward with the sequence, such as:*

EB: "This remaining pain in my body, mind, and heart"
SE: "I choose to let it go"
UE: "This remaining stress, anger, and fear in my body, mind, and heart"
UN: "I choose to let it go"
CH: "No, I can't"
CB: "Yes, I can"
UA: "I don't know if it's possible to feel good"
LV: "Maybe it is, but not right now"
WR: "If not now, then when?"
CR: "Maybe next year"

EB:   "What—next year?!?"
SE:   "Oh, that's too long from now"
UE:   "Maybe I'll let go of my pain and discomfort in nine months" (six months; three months)
UN:   "Maybe I'll let go of my stress, anger, and fear in nine months" (six months; three months)
CH:   "That sounds good"
CB:   "No, it doesn't"
UA:   "Yes, it does"
LV:   "I need to stew a bit longer"
WR:   "I'll postpone having hope until nine months from now" (six months; three months)
CR:   "And I won't laugh until nine months from now" (six months; three months)
EB:   "That sounds like a reasonable plan"
SE:   "No it doesn't"
UE:   "Yes, it does"
UN:   "No, I want to start *now*"
CH:   "Letting go of anger and fear *now*"
CB:   "And I choose to have some hope *now*"
UA:   "And laugh whenever I can, like *now*"
LV:   "I choose to embrace my insides and outsides"
WR:   "Without judgment"
CR:   "Because I deeply and completely love and accept myself" ❃

Take a DEEP breath, drink water, and relax.

❖   CHOICE Statement: KC: "I *choose* to expand the energy within my body and envision my powerful heart in action, so that I may glow with vibrancy and confidence. Thank you, Universe, for *allowing* my inner light to attract beautiful opportunities, *nourishing* my body, heart, and soul with vibrant energy, and *empowering* me to be of service to myself and others. And I deeply and completely love and accept myself." ∞

*Note: Slowly repeat the above CHOICE statement three times before moving forward with the venting sequence, such as:*

EB: "I choose to expand"
SE: "Expand the energy inside my body"
UE: "And let it flow freely with ease"
UN: "I choose to envision"
CH: "Envision my powerful heart"
CB: "Beating strong with purpose"
UA: "Free from all distractions"
LV: "And free to take action"
WR: "I know I glow"
CR: "Because of my heart"
EB: "It takes great responsibility"
SE: "For carrying the rest of my body"
UE: "I thank you, heart"
UN: "For helping me glow"
CH: "With vibrancy and confidence"
CB: "To the best of your ability"
UA: "I honor you"
LV: "And salute you"
WR: "For supporting my breath"
CR: "My brain"
EB: "And my blood"

SE:  "Thank you, Universe"

UE:  "For nourishing my inner light"

UN:  "And allowing it to attract beautiful opportunities"

CH:  "For feeding my body, heart, and soul"

CB:  "And for empowering me to serve from my heart" ❧

Take a DEEP breath, drink water, and relax. Assess how your body is feeling. Thank you for your wonderful efforts. Reach out to people you trust for support and celebration!

*\*Pro EFT™ (Progressive Energy Field Tapping™) and the tool "Reversal Neutralization" were developed by EFT Master Lindsay Kenny.*

*\*\*Note to EFT and Pro EFT practitioners and mental health professionals. Although my story of personal transformation is the focus of this book, you can look forward to a forthcoming clinical (yet lively) workbook and workshop that dives more deeply into many of the complex issues I bring to light. Thank you for dedicating your life to bringing relief to people living with chronic pain, illness, or addiction, as well as those who love and care for them.*

*\*\*\*You may wish to fill in a couple of your own possible reasons in any of these passages.*

# APPENDIX C:

## List of 26 Self-Care Vigilante™ Affirmations

1. Love Every Part: *"I love myself and every part of my body."* ❧ (p. 187)

2. Cleanse: *"I feed my body and soul ingredients that cleanse anything that does not belong in me."* ❧ (p. 189)

3. Laugh: *"I laugh to pee-point every single day."* ❧ (p. 190)

4. F.L.O.W.: *"I look for the positive messages of light in every challenging situation."* ❧ (p. 191)

5. Give Permission: *"I give myself permission to be human and embrace my imperfect ways."* ❧ (p. 193)

6. Invite Power: *"I invite a power that is greater than myself to heal me inside and out."* ❧ (p. 194)

7. Be Vibrant: *"I release heavy energy and replace it with vibrant energy."* ❧ (p. 195)

8. Keep Intestines Happy: *"I love, support, and grow all the good bacteria in my gut."* ❧ (p. 196)

9. Embrace Oneness: *"I embrace my connection to the Universe and everyone in it."* ❧ (p. 197)

10. Change Glasses: *"I change my perspective or 'my glasses' whenever I feel stuck and willingly do things differently."* ☙ (p. 198)

11. Welcome Water: *"I thrive on growing, evolving, and changing continuously."* ☙ (p. 200)

12. Shine with Role Models: *"I surround myself with people who shine in their power, and I welcome their support."* ☙ (p. 201)

13. Rise and Soar: *"I gather the best tools from every personal development program and shape them for me."* ☙ (p. 202)

14. Lean Forward: *"I lean forward to listen, learn, and engage."* ☙ (p. 204)

15. Focus on Good: *"I focus on all the good in my life and have confidence I can create more of it and flourish."* ☙ (p. 205)

16. Live Authentically: *"I show what I feel and embrace honesty and authenticity."* ☙ (p. 207)

17. Embrace Time: *"I connect ideas, energy, and solutions wherever I go."* ☙ (p. 208)

18. Give a Voice: *"I tap into my subconscious mind and give it the voice it deserves to have."* ☙ (p. 209)

19. Acknowledge Polarity: *"I embrace dark and light sides within me and allow both to work for me."* ೞ (p. 210)

20. Dissolve Judgment: *"I dissolve sarcastic and judgmental thoughts instantaneously."* ೞ (p. 211)

21. Seek Mission: *"I accept my presence and mission on this planet."* ೞ (p. 212)

22. Celebrate Inner Light: *"I see my light and celebrate its power to bring relief to others."* ೞ (p. 214)

23. Find Serious Humor: *"I find humor in my past and in my non-traditional ways."* ೞ (p. 215)

24. Protect Inner Flame: *"I detach from whatever dims my inner flame."* ೞ (p. 216)

25. Forgive: *"I forgive myself and everyone who is unavailable or unable to help me grow stronger and upward."* ೞ (p. 218)

26. Serve with a Full Cup: *"I give to others when my cup is full, because I am a Self-Care Vigilante!"* ೞ (p. 219)

Visit www.fieldofchoices.com for a free mini-poster of all 26 Self-Care Vigilante Affirmations when you sign up for the newsletter.

# Praise for

## Tap into the Universe for Recovery, Book 1:

### Birth of a Self-Care Vigilante

"Reading about Ilana Kristeva's crazy journey will give even the most affected by chronic pain (like myself) real hope for exciting new possibilities. I strongly believe that anyone feeling as though they are 'stuck' in their position in life could benefit greatly from her book. It is not only a joy to read, but the endorphins from laughing alone can't help but make you feel better! I love her description of vibrancy: 'The glow of the dancing flame in our soul that shines within us so brightly that people can see it from the outside.' She is able to generate vibrancy, inspiration, and excitement in me—and it feels fantastic!"

—Tara White, R.N., B.S.N., CRPS survivor, and Facilitator for the Sacramento Chapter of the American Chronic Pain Association (ACPA)

"Ilana's passion for life and amazing energy really shine through in this book. I think that her candor, warmth, and tenacity will inspire others who have struggled with their health to move forward with hope and optimism. With tremendous determination to prevail, she overcame multiple layers of trauma to reclaim her life. Her willingness to be

vulnerable by sharing her story, just to help others, is truly a gift to the world."
　　—Lindsay Kenny, EFT Master and Founder of the Pro EFT Institute

"I found the book to have remarkable purity, revealing authentic insight into the mind and spirit of a person with chronic pain. This is a book of hope for the person suffering with chronic pain and offers insight to the people who care. Ilana Kristeva is rightfully unapologetic for being herself, as she is both unique and universal at the same time."
　　—Dr. William J. Conard, M.D., Asclepius Pain Management; Developer of the "Asclepius Complete Care Model," integrating principles of Functional Medicine with BioMedical and BioPsychoSocial pain treatment models

"For those of us desirous of healing, and that can be from the base of all the spirals we traverse, Ilana's book is perfect. How she humorously shares her journey and invites us in interactively are some of her unique offerings, including her generous sharing of *7 Key Ingredients for Vibrancy* and her *26 Self-Care Vigilante Affirmations*—all truly outstanding! I will be suggesting this easy while profound read to my clients for inspiration and practical tapping affirmations."
　　—Suzanne D. Alfandari, M.S., L.M.F.T., Expert Certified EFT Practitioner and member of Motivational Interviewing Network of Trainers (MINT)

"Having treated many patients with chronic and degenerative conditions, I found that most are unable to get out of the unconscious patterns that have created their illnesses. This story offers much hope to those who suffer. I enjoyed Ilana's quirky, nerdy, and deeply profound story of pain, suffering, awakening, and recovery and loved her take on many principles: surrender, acceptance, forgiveness, and the beautiful art of practicing gratitude. Thank you for sharing your journey and your humor with the world."

—Dr. Sean Patterson, D.C., Founder of Body Restore, trainer, lecturer, author of *The Pre Diet Plan—Everything That Must Happen Before You Can Successfully Diet to Lose Weight*, and radio personality on Money105.5's *Health & Money*

"In its simultaneous humanness and practicality, this heartfelt, humble, and humorous guided tour of Ilana's journey is captivating to me as a person and as a clinical psychologist and former nurse-midwife. The mindfulness meditation and adapted-Pro EFT passages are truly beautiful and filled with compassion. I found myself implementing some of the techniques for myself, as well as sharing them with clients. This is a book to refer to again and again, for anyone facing health challenges and those wishing to enhance their well-being and self-care."

—Elizabeth Vitale, M.S.N., Psy.D., psychologist with Psychotherapy Partners, LLC

"I feel my life has been blessed by this book. Ilana's beautifully crafted words capture the reality of what challenges the human spirit can endure while dealing with unrelenting pain. Physical pain, emotional pain, and spiritual pain form a triad that exists for many, though there is no diagnostic code to cover all its depths. She offers her razor-sharp humor and loving compassion as a way through to the other side of triumph and peace; her tangible humane teachings shine a light on a future of peace, enthusiasm, and dignity—all the while choosing the joy of laughter.

A devoted fan of EFT and Pro EFT, I love the way Ilana leads us in tapping sequences that speak to the heart of the raw emotions and confusion of finding ourselves where we are in our lives; how we can reset our situation and battle against giving up the very things that continue our injuries to body, mind, or spirit; and how boldly choosing to move ourselves into peace and healing can become a reality—offering an outcome that equals serenity and triumph as a future reality. *Birth of a Self-Care Vigilante* is a delightful and wonderful contribution to the healing of the reader. Bless you, Ilana, for such a wonderful gift of your talents."

—Nancy J. Yilk, Integrative Health Consultant, Founder of Optimum Health, and integrative medical science writer, *Medical-Surgical Nursing ($2^{nd}$ Edition)* with Kathleen S. Osborn (Author), Cheryl E. Wraa (Author), Annita S. Watson (Author), Renee S. Holleran (Author)

ACKNOWLEDGEMENTS

I would like to acknowledge several significant angels, in human form and on this planet we call Earth, who made it possible for me to write this book for you.

Joe Sweet showed me, by his example, how to transform pain and trauma into service to others, no matter what physical or mental diagnoses are thrown at us. Light shall prevail.

Carol Garner taught me how to laugh and cry through the most incredulous realities I faced, especially while caring for my mother in three hospitals and one skilled-nursing facility during the writing of this book. Shine through storms.

Richard Broadhurst generously coached me in bringing out the best of my assets and shortcomings onto paper and into the limelight. Celebrate humanity.

Lynn Kennedy Baxter revealed my tremendous ability to live on the edge of discovery and thrive outside of my comfort zones as a writer, practitioner, and leader. Follow priorities.

Sharon Araki and Lino Cedros guided my body to homeostasis, showing me that my body could work out its problems—even under the stress of writing and publishing this manuscript—with the combination of my own effort and the support of highly intuitive therapists. Humpty Dumpty can smile again.

Lindsay Kenny, Dr. William Conard, Dr. Sean Patterson, Tara White, Elizabeth Vitale, Suzanne Alfandari, and Nancy J. Yilk spent precious time and energy in reading my book manuscript and then offered their professional review. Thank you for your trust in me to support your patients and clients in their journeys. Connect soul to soul.

And finally, but most importantly, my husband (who wishes to remain anonymous). A special "thank you" to the silliest-wisest man who intu-itively knew when to sit back and when to join me in my moments of constipation—physical, mental, emotional, or spiritual—during the nearly two years of creating this book. Always embrace joy!

# About the Author

Ilana Kristeva, M.P.A., is an out-of-the-box proponent of self-care practices that honor profound wisdom from a wide spectrum of healing modalities— West to East and new to ancient. An author, speaker, and Vibrance Coach, she promotes public awareness of health and safety issues through speaking engagements, books, and Pro EFT "tapping" and Chi Gong sessions. Most importantly, this Self-Care Vigilante manages her chronic systemic disease— Complex Regional Pain Syndrome (CRPS)—and other serious health conditions with grace, ease, and laughter. In her spare time, Ilana performs Self-Care Comedy™ and coaches the Boston Red Sox from the middle of her living room floor.

*Reprinted with permission from RSDHope.org*

Complex Regional Pain Syndrome (CRPS)